4

A Hatful of Pain

CRAIG BURTON

Noble House
Baltimore, Maryland

A Hatful of Pain

Library of Congress
Cataloging in Publication Data
ISBN 1-56167-470-2

Library of Congress Card Catalog Number:
98-86797

Published by

Noble House

8019 Belair Road, Suite 10
Baltimore, Maryland 21236

Manufactured in the United States of America

Disclaimers:

This book is for people who want to be unpopular, unadjusted, unsuccessful, and fat—and who want to read a book for entertainment alone.

While some of the characters in this novel are real, any resemblance to actual persons, living or dead, would totally baffle my English teachers.

You may choose to believe the events in this novel are not real, and that twenty million animals are not tortured annually in U.S. laboratories to test household and cosmetic products. That there is no Animal Liberation Front. And there is no book in your hands.

World wide activities of the Animal Liberation Front and other animal-rights web sites > > http://www.:
- ♦ envirolink.org/alf/orgs.html (Animal Liberation Front)
- ♦ paws.org (Progressive Animal Welfare Society)
- ♦ peta-online.org/index.html (People for the Ethical Treatment of Animals)
- ♦ envirolink.org/arrs (Animal Rights Resource Site)

Grateful acknowledgment is made for permission to reprint lyrics from the following songs:

"Tame Yourself," by Raw Youth. Copyright 1991 P.E.T.A. All rights reserved. Used by permission.

"Slaves." Words by Hope Nicholls, music by Fetchin Bones. Copyright 1991 P.E.T.A. All rights reserved. Used by permission.

"Don't Be Part Of It," by Howard Jones. All rights reserved. Used by permission.

Editing everthng except but this sentence did by Haven Books International, P.O. Box 950, Camarillo, CA, 93011.

The pages are numbered backwards because the author thinks people prefer to know how many pages they have left. He may be wrong about this. He has been wrong about other things.

A Hatful of Pain

Debts:

To my wife, Karen—I owe my joy. She has always had my respect, will always have my love, and will always be my friend.

To my dad—I owe what I am. He influenced me to become a more decent human being than I ever really wanted.

To other creditors—the total is $17,621.
Thanks, gentlemen.

<u>Reviews of "A Hatful of Pain"</u>

"It is quite entertaining and the message is certainly spot on!"
   —**Ingrid Newkirk**, *co-founder of People for the Ethical Treatment of Animals*

"Action-packed and sidesplitting . . ."
   —**Dorothy S. Stein**, author of *An Ordinary Obsession*

"Unique. Always funny and smart, it vacillates from cartoonish, to romantic, to dramatic, to strange combinations of all three."
   —**Dr. Stanley Roberts**, author of *Mind Twist*

"If you have only enough time to read one book, I recommend this one! I read it twice."
   —**Joan Hannefeld**, author of *My Enemies Are Naked*

"It's hard to laugh and cry at the same time, but this is just that kind of book."
   —**Martha Mason**, editor of *Detective Files*

"This book reminds me of *M*A*S*H*—comedy in the grimmest of circumstances. Humor necessary for the sake of sanity."
   —**Christopher Allen**

"If a group of beings from another planet were to land on Earth—beings who considered themselves as superior to you as you feel yourself to be to other animals—would you concede them the rights over you that you assume over other animals?"
George Bernard Shaw, *playwright, Nobel 1925*

"I must interpret the life about me as I interpret the life that is my own. My life is full of meaning to me. The life around me must be full of significance to itself. If I am to expect others to respect my life, then I must respect the other life I see, however strange it may be to mine. . . . We need a boundless ethics which will include the animals also."
Dr. Albert Schweitzer, *Civilization and Ethics, Nobel 1952*

"I am in favor of animal rights as well as human rights. That is the way of a whole human being."
Abraham Lincoln, *16th U.S. President*

"The greatness of a nation and its moral progress can be judged by the way its animals are treated."
Mahatma Gandhi, *statesman and philosopher*

"Our task must be to free ourselves . . . by widening our circle of compassion to embrace all living creatures and the whole of nature and its beauty."
Albert Einstein, *physicist, Nobel 1921*

"Until we stop harming all other living beings, we are still savages."
Thomas Jefferson, *3rd U.S. President*

"You have just dined, and however scrupulously the slaughterhouse is concealed in the graceful distance of miles, there is complicity."
Ralph Waldo Emerson, *author*

"As long as there are slaughterhouses, there will be battle-fields."
Leo Tolstoy, *author*

"For as long as men massacre animals, they will kill each other. Indeed, he who sows the seed of murder and pain cannot reap joy and love."
Pythagoras, *mathematician*

"I am not interested to know whether vivisection produces results that are profitable to the human race or doesn't. . . . The pain which it inflicts upon unconsenting animals is the basis of my enmity toward it, and it is to me sufficient justification of the enmity without looking further."
Mark Twain, *author*

"In their behavior toward creatures, all men are Nazis. Human beings see oppression vividly when they're the victims. Otherwise they victimize blindly and without a thought."
Isaac Bashevis Singer, *author, Nobel 1978*

"[The day should come when] all of the forms of life . . . will stand before the court—the pileated woodpecker as well as the coyote and bear, the lemmings as well as the trout in the streams."
William O. Douglas, *late U.S. Supreme Court Justice*

"The time will come when men such as I will look upon the murder of animals as they now look on the murder of men."
Leonardo da Vinci, *artist and scientist*

"If there is no struggle, there is no progress. Those who profess to favour freedom, and yet deprecate agitation, are people who want rain without thunder and lightning. They want the ocean without the roar of its many waters. Power concedes nothing without a demand. It never did and it never will."
Frederick Douglass, *slavery abolitionist*

"I say, break the law."
Henry David Thoreau, *essayist and poet*

I drove the van slowly, scanning the street signs reflected in my headlights. Behind me, ragged dark clouds flew like witches among faint stars and a thin moon. I was just ahead of a snowstorm that hadn't been predicted, and its flashes of lightning sparked a danger sign in my mind.

I cut the headlights, cut the motor, and coasted to a stop across the street from the Mischievous Motel. The three-story building sat between a deserted pool hall and a run-down tenement.

I pulled my wig down just over my forehead, topped it with a Boston Red Sox cap, and double-checked the contents of my paper bag.

After a brewery truck rumbled by, I stepped out of the van to an audience of eight or nine kids sneering and making wisecracks. I felt them sizing me up.

I'm six-one and was a varsity wrestler for Boston College, but my slight limp and baby face don't exude the authority necessary for survival in dark alleys, rough bars, or newly opened express checkout lanes.

"Hey, thanks for the van."

"Washing it should disguise it."

"Don't hurry back."

I couldn't let the kids distract me. I dashed across the icy street, fighting the wind.

When I passed the darkened entrance of Hammer's Pool Hall, I tripped over the legs of a man sitting on the cold pavement. He was propped against a bent metal grocery cart full of garbage bags. His pockets were turned inside out. He didn't bother to look up.

I hesitated over him, feeling a strange bond between us, a peculiar sort of camaraderie. Yes, my clothes appeared to have some pharmaceutical explanation—but it was more than that. In him I saw an image of every outsider who'd ever lived, myself included. Outsiders hoping someday it might occur to the general populace, perhaps while they're stepping over some man on the sidewalk who could soon be lying in the ragged coffin of his own frozen body, that the system just may not be working.

I set down my paper bag, pulled out my wallet and dropped all my cash—forty dollars—into his lap. I was encouraged when he stuffed the bills into his shirt pocket (recently a homeless lady had taken a bill from me, stuffed it into her moist mouth, and chewed it with salivating relish). The man looked up, mouth ajar, eyes wet. I think he'd been crying. He couldn't have been much older than me, maybe thirty, but he looked like a very old man.

If he could have endured any eye-to-eye contact, he might have taken the chance and smiled at me. As it was, he nodded slightly and returned his gaze to the ground.

"I'll be back soon." *I have to go. Honest.*

I picked up my paper bag and stepped around him. Before heading into the alley I checked my watch. 11:59:30. In thirty seconds a homeless-looking man should give me a signal.

Fifty yards ahead of me a man with an overcoat buttoned up to his chin staggered into a trashcan. I think he said,

"Excuse me, ma'am." Two women in miniskirts and fur coats who'd been loitering on the corner approached him. One of them gave him something. I waited for him to signal to me, but instead he shuffled away. 12:01:18. Something was wrong.

Backing into the shadows, I looked toward the man sitting in the entrance of the pool hall. Surely he wasn't the operative. But who else could it be?

I peered into the shadows of the alley one last time. A human figure was emerging and straightening from what a moment before had appeared to be only a large pile of trash. He brushed himself off, then nodded at me.

I signaled to a solitary figure pacing on the roof of the tenement, then headed into the alley between a battered hurricane fence and the motel. Several windows were lit. In one, a woman wearing only a red lace brassiere was sitting on the lap of a man in a Santa Claus costume. I ducked and ran past it.

Sixty yards into the alley I flexed my fingers and tugged on the frosted railing of a fire escape. It felt sturdy. I hoped so. All I could see to break my fall were greasy fast-food wrappers swirling after each other.

The large paper bag clenched between my teeth made climbing awkward. Two stories up, I slipped on an icy rung. Dangling by my arms in the wind, all my muscles tightened— my hands so I wouldn't fall, my jaw so I wouldn't drop the bag, my sphincter so I wouldn't soil my pants. Finally, I found the rung with my feet and kept going.

As I pulled myself up onto the snowy roof, I inhaled a mouthful of stale frying fat fumes billowing from the exhaust of the motel's coffee shop. I worked my way through the smoke and across the slippery roof to the far edge. Keeping my eyes on the horizon, I took a walkie-talkie from my pocket and checked its channel.

Next, I pulled out my binoculars. Three miles east, I saw the Atlantic Ocean. Moving slowly, the top of the mast of a cargo iceboat disappeared behind the golden steeple of a church. I focused on the Terrig Corporation Animal Test Lab, one block down Terrig Street. Next, I scouted for police cars. I saw fire escapes of nearby buildings, and a beer sign's blinking yellow light. In the distance, dark purple clouds marked a rapidly moving squall line.

I checked my watch—forty seconds left. No time to figure out what complications the storm might bring. I keyed my walkie-talkie.

"Van one."

Slowly, a white van pulled around the corner. Black lettering stenciled on its rear doors read ABC LAUNDRY SERVICE. It stopped in front of the Terrig Test Lab and two operatives sprang out. Lab coats and sanitary face masks disguised them as laboratory technicians. Using a key, they entered the building through the front door.

I blew on my icy fingertips, then focused the binoculars on the van. The rear doors opened. A ramp lowered. An operative wheeled an industrial-size laundry cart down the ramp, onto the street, and into the Test Lab at a pace suggesting more at stake than brighter whites.

I continued watching the cross streets. Four rumpled men sat on a snow-cleared curb warming themselves in steam rising from a sewer grating.

Wind slapped at my jacket. I waited for the operative to return.

Two minutes later, he came out of the lab pushing the cart slowly. My binoculars revealed a full cargo of bloody lab coats. From beneath the coats, cries of fear carried in the wind and stirred rage that rippled along my spine. I rubbed the back of my neck, massaging the knots my muscles had twisted themselves into.

From inside the van an assistant emerged and pulled the heavy cart slowly up the ramp. The operative raced another empty cart down the ramp and into the Test Lab. A few minutes later, puffing hard into the frigid air, he returned with the second cart full.

The van drove away leaving two operatives inside the lab. Sixty seconds later, I keyed the walkie-talkie.

"Two!"

A second van, twin to the first, arrived from the opposite direction. Two more laundry carts were shuttled in. I moved carefully across the roof. My van was surrounded by kids with tattoos, boot camp haircuts, and broken-glass expressions, casually plotting their lives of crime.

Snow started falling. I wiped moisture from the binoculars and scanned the streets. One block north, as out of place as a ski mask in a bank, was a late model car. A white Toyota. Braking repeatedly, its driver rapidly twisted his head left and right, perhaps aware that if he turned down the wrong street, his car and he would be spare parts and Alpo before he could shift into reverse. From my perch, the car looked like a white rat lost in a maze.

Two vans had come and gone without incident and a third identical van arrived as the wind swung to the north. With the changing wind, new sounds emerged from the night. Swirling in their center was the wail of a police siren. Sirens were part of the music of the city, day and night, but this was close.

Headlights broke the darkness of Terrig Street. I keyed my walkie-talkie.

"Hold still."

"Tell it," a voice huffed. "Tell it fast." In the background I heard metal cages being pried open.

"Hazard one," I said, then cued my brother stationed on the far side of Terrig, "Diversion A. Hit it."

"Ten-four."

A police cruiser, lights flashing, rolled up behind the van. I hoped that the operatives in the van wouldn't resist arrest, but they might. Perhaps they hadn't learned, as I did two years ago, to put your hands on top of your head to avoid the unpleasant experience of getting shot first and questioned afterward.

My resultant limp is almost gone. However, my leg ached a little in tonight's cold.

A hand-held searchlight from the police cruiser shone on the license plate of the van. Suddenly, a burglar alarm began shrieking. The cruiser pulled around the van, fishtailed slightly, then raced away.

Diversion 'A', never before attempted, had worked.

During the loading of the eighth and final van, snow began falling faster. The connection between the unforeseen snow and impending danger flashed once more across my mind.

Water-based paint.

I snapped the binoculars to my eyes and focused on the rear doors of the van. The "Y" of ABC LAUNDRY was dripping. I focused on the license plate. The "E" was bleeding, changing back to its original "L."

Police backup was surely on the way. We had to get the van out of there.

Too late! The piercing sound of a police siren tied a knot in my stomach. I keyed my walkie-talkie.

"Second hazard one."

No answer.

A cruiser turned down Terrig Street. As it slowed, the pitch of its engine lowered. It sounded hungry. Feral.

I panicked and ignored code. "Police. Hold still."

No answer.

I pressed the cold metal receiver against my forehead to keep from yelling into it. The cruiser's headlights were diffused by snow that seemed not to be reflecting light but glowing with a radiance of its own.

Answer!

"Ten-four," a soft female voice said. Kristin. Good. She wouldn't make any mistakes. Although only twenty years old, she was an experienced operative.

The cruiser's searchlight lit up as the car rolled to a stop directly behind the van. The beam shone on the van's rear doors, then traced the paint flowing downward in river patterns.

The light flicked off, the doors opened, and two giant cops wearing yellow rain ponchos climbed out of the cruiser and stalked the van. They looked as if they could lift it off the ground and play catch with it.

"Team three: start Diversion B in sixty seconds."

I would need the full minute. I hoped Kristin would wait inside the lab and perfectly time her escape—and that the driver of the van wouldn't panic and leave without her.

I reached into my paper bag and removed a radio-controlled model Cobra helicopter. I positioned it on the roof, then checked its payload. Muted by a Whisper Tech muffler, its engine wouldn't be heard above the wind and the rattling of the coffee shop's exhaust fan. After testing the controls, I lifted it off. Stabilized by a gyro, it rose twenty yards straight up, then propelled forward into the threatening sky.

As I zeroed it in on a final approach down Terrig Street, the wind rocked it hard. I struggled to keep it upright. The Cobra had to be steady when its bay doors opened or it would shake and lose altitude. Impatient, I kept shifting the controls from one hand to the other, fingering the button that releases the payload.

One of the cops peered in the rear window of the van. H is partner took off a glove, then w iped at the ▓ABC." Moving decisively now, he shoved his glove back on and began rounding the van, shouting something that made his partner start going around the far side.

Cutting the speed of the Cobra, I maneuvered it into position less than a yard above the police cruiser. From that point, I lifted it straight up about fifty yards and stabilized the controls. When the Cobra seemed steady, I released the payload. Two dozen clear glass marbles rained down on the metal trunk.

Bang! Bang! Bang!

Even a block away it sounded like gunfire.

Both cops spun, drew their guns, and went into a crouch, frantically yelling things I couldn't make out. They crouch-hopped toward the cruiser, springing up and down as if riding short, invisible ponies, waving guns in all directions.

I keyed my walkie-talkie. It triggered a gunshot that rang in the distance.

The cops scrambled into the cruiser, U-turned, and drove down Terrig Street shining their light into every dark corner along the way.

Unhindered, the van drove off.

I worked the next several minutes bringing the Cobra in to a safe landing. Then I returned to the edge of the icy roof.

I had not seen Kristin escape. *Maybe she slipped away while I was landing the Cobra.* I keyed my mike.

"Everybody okay?"

A popping noise came through the speaker, followed by the chugging sound of the van's engine. The driver's voice held a rasp of excitement. "Smashing aerial show, Captain. Thanks for pulling my chestnuts out of the fire."

The unexpected humor loosened the knot in my stomach.

"You're welcome. Is everyone accounted for?"

No answer.

I repeated my question.

Again no answer.

I thumped the walkie-talkie to make sure the batteries were in place.

"Got everybody?"

Still no answer. The night suddenly seemed darker and colder.

The silence was broken by the shriek of skidding tires. The police cruiser with the cops in yellow ponchos was rounding the corner and it squealed to a halt in front of Terrig Corporation.

After charging out of the cruiser the cops stared open-mouthed at the spot where the van had been parked minutes before. Then they jumped along the street, kicking at slush puddles and flapping like giant yellow bats.

I waited. The storm blackened the sky. The golden steeple of the church went monochromatic before disappearing altogether.

After the cops finally left, I climbed down the fire escape.

Keeping a wary eye on the shadows, I made my way through the alley, then onto the slushy sidewalk. Wind lashed the snow in waves. I glanced toward Hammer's Pool Hall and hesitated. I felt bad about not returning to the homeless man in the entranceway.

I'll help him later. Something seemed to have gone wrong with the mission. Head down, I crossed the street.

All four tires of my van were still inflated, and all the hubcaps were still there. The gang hadn't been feeling playful.

They were, however, watching me like buzzards watch a dying horse crossing the desert. One thin punk, his face decorated as if he'd just removed it from a tackle box, was leaning on the van. Behind me, someone shouted a nasty anatomical name popular with guys who like to sound tough.

I kept walking. Did they think I had money? Was I on their turf?

From every direction, I heard whistles and movement. The gang was mobilizing. Shit creek seemed to have claimed me. A paddle wouldn't help.

The gang was almost on me. I saw glints of reflected light and heard Switchblades snicking open.

I ran, anticipating the punk leaning on the van would block my path.

Ghostlike, he went backward, fusing into shadows.

I didn't realize how relieved I was to reach my van until I climbed inside and was overcome with emotion and the yearning to softly kiss my steering wheel. Then came the sinking feeling the gang's calmness was due to their knowledge that my van's engine was resting on the sidewalk behind them. And I wasn't going anywhere.

I ground the starter, gave the engine too much gas, and was surprised when it growled to life somewhere under a cloud of smoke. I wasn't sure whether the engine was running or on fire, but I put it in gear.

Curious about why the gang had let me go, I rolled down my window and looked back. The gang was skillfully melding into the night, and racing toward me was a carnival of whirling red and white lights.

I slid down in the front seat until my knees banged against the dashboard. The approaching headlights briefly swept across the interior above me, then raced by, heading toward Terrig Street.

After they rounded the corner, I sat up and tried the walkie-talkie. Still no response.

I drove eight blocks in the opposite direction, parked, got out, and backtracked on foot. Wind whipped at my face. I plunged my hands into my pockets and walked briskly past boarded up buildings, an empty Laundromat, and a gun shop advertising a "Back to School" special.

A hundred yards farther, in the middle of an otherwise vacant block, I reached a fence surrounding a U-Rent Storage compound. I stopped and looked over my shoulder in the traditionally furtive fashion of someone about to do something illegal. Then I climbed the fence, dropped to the other side, and trotted to the back, where the aisle was barricaded by a rusted out car sitting on concrete blocks. The car didn't have an interior, and just junk where the engine had been.

Two men were pounding on the car with heavy tools, their noise barely masking the growling and barking coming from the storage shed beyond. Ten feet from the old car, I stopped. I suspected the men knew I was there, but they didn't look up.

I moved closer.

A man with a face like a constipated bulldog's stopped and stepped out to block my path. Threatening. His hands curled into fists, his lip into a snarl. Primal and deadly.

I forgot the password.

"Gulp."

That wasn't it.

He took a step toward me.

"Eat beans," I stammered, "not beings."

He smiled and I could see what he'd looked like as a little kid. Quickly he was behind me, slapping me soundly between the shoulders—which started me stumbling through a maze of crushed automobile parts.

Exiting the maze, I crawled through the side door of an ABC LAUNDRY van, out the back, and into a storage shed. In the center of the shed a light bulb tucked into a dented metal cone hung from the ceiling. Directly below the cone, a folding card table stood like an island in a sea of dog cages, laundry carts, and other supplies and equipment.

Squeezed around the periphery of the shed were twenty operatives wearing lab coats, tailored, it seemed, by the same guy who designed the Hefty Bag. The coats were accessorized with cheap wigs and fake mustaches.

I looked for Kristin, who I'd recognize in any disguise. We'd been teammates on many missions of the Animal Liberation Front. Blonde and pixyish, it was the passion of Kristin's gaze that made her memorable; her beauty sprang from her soul and illuminated her physical features.

But she wasn't here. I wondered if anybody had seen her, my brother, or the driver of the final van. But no trained operative would admit they knew anything about lookouts, drivers, or for that matter, the person standing next to him.

The guy right next to me spoke. "We're awfully close to Terrig."

"If the cops find us here," I said, "I'll be very surprised."

"We'll all be surprised," he said. "Unpleasantly."

I turned my attention to the two men and two women nearest the table. The men, veterinarians, were scrambling to set up shop. One of the two women was my sister, Corky.

Corky was the liaison between the A.L.F. and my rock band, Fluke. A third-grade school teacher, she would be my candidate for the person best qualified to run the universe, should that office ever get on the ballot. She had only a small repertoire of movements, brief and exact, like her words.

Standing next to her, with sparkling green eyes set in a sprinkle of freckles, was Ann Berlin, lead singer and saxophonist of Fluke. Her black jeans were tucked into black boots. A shifting curtain of blonde hair gathered loosely into the collar of her black coat. She had a law degree, and always tried to help people, but dressed in all black she looked intimidating. Dangerous even.

Corky raised her head slightly and gathered everyone's eyes.

"Don't take off your disguises. Talk only if you have to. Dogs with life-threatening wounds are our top priority. Bring them to this table. Dogs with no hope for survival will be put to sleep." Her eyes added, "Go!"

Inside the pen to my right a small brown puppy lay on his back, paws up, tongue out the side of his mouth, whimpering. The burns on his sides were raw, bleeding, festering. Kneeling down, I scratched his belly. His face was swollen.

"You'll be okay."

His tail wagged weakly in reply. Somehow he still wanted to trust mankind after all we'd done to him.

"Good boy."

Although he could hardly roll over, he struggled up, tried

to lick my hand, looked embarrassed and promptly collapsed in a heap. I scratched his ears, lifted him out, and cradled him close to my chest. He managed to lick my chin.

The younger of the two vets wore a folded bandanna around his head that looked like a cardinal in flight. He signaled I was next.

The older vet was the gentle grandfatherly type. If they'd been making a movie and looking for a small-town vet, he would have been perfect casting. Cold air had tinged his skin light blue. He slid over to the portable heater and held out his shivering hands—hands that needed to be steady.

The young vet removed rubber gloves from a medical bag. "Here, Dr. Dean . . ." His voice trailed away as he realized he'd breached the confidentiality essential to the Animal Liberation Front, since the FBI lists us as a terrorist organization.

"Excuse me?" I said, pretending I thought he'd been talking to me and I hadn't heard him clearly. The young vet's eyes thanked me.

I set the puppy gently on the table. As the two vets examined him, he lay silent, head on his paws, looking up at me. He opened his mouth slightly, then closed it, as though forever.

"They'll fix you up," I said. He wiggled his tail once, weakly.

After a few moments Dr. Dean shook his head and took out a needle. I knew what that meant. So quickly extinguished was my spark of hope. Eyes open, staring ahead, the small brown puppy looked as he had an instant ago. For something as meaningful as it is, death doesn't look like much at first.

A slow blues riff ran through my mind, an all-too-familiar theme. Regret. *We should've gotten to Terrig sooner.*

Once again, Corky drew everyone's attention. As before, it was her stillness you noticed, the economy of movement emphasized by the way she did not speak, but politely waited.

"Second priority," she said. "Calm any barking dogs who might give away our location. Third: examine dogs in pain. Fourth: feed each dog. Finally: return the vans to the rental agencies and discard all the clothes you wore tonight. Fibers can be used to link you to the Terrig Lab." She paused as the sound of sirens grew louder. When they began fading, she continued. "We'll guard this shed in six-hour shifts. In three days, if the police have let up on their search, we'll take the dogs to the Peace Plantation Refuge."

They'd be safe there.

Memories of the thousand acre Refuge, some as vivid as photographs, flipped through my mind. Once, while I was working there, an elderly woman returned to thank us, saying that when we saved a small dog from destruction and gave it to her, we had saved two lives. She claimed that Winnie the Pooch provided her with the most unselfish love she'd ever experienced. He gratefully slept on the cold ground to be near her, licked her hand even when she had no food to offer, guarded her as though she were royalty. Gave her a reason to live.

I hoped that some of the dogs rescued tonight would one day have a similar impact.

I moved to a snarling little bundle of ferocity, a Scottish terrier, and held out my hand. He growled, sniffed, then allowed me to pat his head.

Two hours later, every dog was fed. Some were asleep. Three were dead.

"Great work," Ann said, to the nods and smiles of everyone in the room.

We had saved eighty-five dogs and filmed video footage of Terrig's illegal animal testing. But our biggest challenge loomed a week ahead. December eighteenth. The Laurel Corporation. But where was Kristin?

Ann looked at Corky.

My sister said, "As you all know, our next mission involves even higher stakes; the lives of over *ten thousand* rabbits. Laurel is trying to extend their government grant for another five years. To get this research welfare, three million dollars' worth, Laurel has only to complete one final battery of tests and file a report. We can stop them by taking photos of signed test procedures that prove they are defrauding the government. We'll contact you in the usual way. Code twelve. Repeat: code *one, two.* Timing will be critical. Take care, and thanks."

One operative left every two minutes. The first to go were those who'd requested to leave early—like Ann Berlin, who worked Sundays for a legal firm providing free services to the poor. Ann represented children in child abuse cases, and her workload increased each year. As a result, the firm put pressure on her to join them full-time. Certainly her legal work was very important, but it seemed to me there were plenty of lawyers to handle all the legitimate work, with some to spare. A.L.F. members were hard to come by. So, every Sunday, I said a silent prayer we wouldn't lose her, and this was the cause of some of my anxiety on weekends. Although, admittedly, some of it was due to the slipshod play of the New England Patriots.

Having no pressing engagements, I was one of the last to leave. I drove back to Hammer's. The same homeless man lay in the doorway, asleep, his legs under his grocery cart. His head rested on the cold cement sidewalk. His neck was at an angle that made me wince. It looked broken. After I saw him breathing, I took off my jacket, folded it, and slid it under his cheek. He didn't awaken.

A vague disquiet lingered, one I'd had since leaving the shed, a nagging sense that I was forgetting something, or unaware of something. *Am I being followed?* Holding down my wig, I peered from the entrance of the pool hall. Winds swept clean the east side of the street, piling deep snowdrifts against the west side. The street was deserted except for a cat that scampered across the sidewalk and hid behind the tire of a parked car, watching me. No people. No traffic.

What's wrong?

Sirens still blared from the direction of the Terrig Lab, which worried me. Why would they still be there? Had they gotten Kristin? I was tempted to return to Terrig, but knew better. I'd been trained to stick to the plan.

My thoughts swirled away from the sirens and sank into my gut. The chilling experience of seeing animals suffering was mingling with the warmth of knowing I'd helped stop some of it. In the morning, Mr. Terrig would be very surprised. And very, very angry. *With no dogs to torture, he might grease the steps at the old folks home.*

I managed a choking laugh. I had to. Laughter kept the lid on my anger.

After spending the day inside the U-Rent Storage shed, my brother Bill and I drove northwest into Cavalry, then to the east side of Cavalry where the graffiti was densest. At first, all that spray painting looked like vandalism. As I got used to it, I realized it gave a bright splash of color to the otherwise drab neighborhood, and that once you got past the prejudice against defacing public property it really wasn't all that bad. Of course, I never said this to anyone.

Amidst that graffiti was a spotless red brick building, its owner managing to have been more persistent than the neighborhood taggers. Not that the building, the Howling Lobster, was free of spray paint. Inside, Bill and I sat at a table under a six-foot-high cartoon spray-painted on the wall. The cartoon depicted a chef about to dump a live lobster into a pot of boiling water on a gas stove. The lobster was saying to the chef, "Just because it's your job, doesn't make it right."

It felt good to be in the Lobster because the memories were good. Our band had held its first gig to support the with the Lobster's crowd of regulars. Now, our concerts were the lifeblood of the A.L.F.'s operating budget.

Bill, twenty-six years old, looked like a young President Clinton with shoulder-length blonde hair. Tonight he wore a religious medallion draped around his neck, which he held away from his chest, watching it unwind on its chain. There was always a restless energy about his movements.

I was bombing in beer nuts and expostulating on topics of cosmic significance, such as how fresh the nuts tasted. I drank water, though alcohol was free. I hoped this would build character, a quality I couldn't afford to pass up, whatever the price. I'd recently turned twenty-seven, and I figured it was now or never on the question of character.

Bill and I talked softly and laughed about how lucky we'd been last night with "Diversion A." To distract the police, Bill had run up and down side streets, rocking parked cars and triggering alarms.

"They almost caught me," he said, "when I stopped to listen to one alarmed car talk to me. It kept saying in a whiny voice, 'I've been tampered with.' Cops tore around the corner and I had to dive through an ice-covered hedge and share a mulberry bush with a hoot owl."

My brother was exaggerating, as he frequently did, creating the image he was slightly crazier than he really was. Crazy or not, his dedication to the A.L.F. continued to surprise me. His strong religious beliefs did not fall in line with the beliefs of animal-rights activists. Deep into God, he believed things that people have difficulty believing even in Salt Lake City. Yet somehow his loyalty to family superseded his loyalty to self. His internal struggle surfaced only occasionally. Although, sometimes without warning.

Bill tilted his head slightly to see past my left shoulder. I shifted enough to follow his gaze. Threading his way toward us, around a small nativity scene and through the crowd, was the owner of the Lobster, Richard Tipton. An accomplished jazz pianist, Richard joined us onstage at our request.

From a distance, he looked like an overweight Bill Cosby. But up close he had the run-over look of a man who was struggling to make ends meet. He had been my father's best friend and they'd played together in a jazz band in Indiana more than two decades ago. Richard would have been like a father to me, if it weren't for the fact he was like a father to so many others.

I didn't like what I saw trailing Richard—a huge bald-headed monster whose face bore shiny white scar tissue that looked as hard as marble. When they reached our table, Richard put his arm around the monster, who smiled as though he'd been scratched behind the ears.

"This is Chas Blat," Richard said. "New bouncer, long-time friend."

Bill and I stood as Richard introduced us. "Chas, meet the Baker brothers. Bill, who always wears a religious medallion, and Clark, who always wears an ear-to-ear grin." He slapped Chas's shoulder. "Between you and me, son, both adornments make me suspect they're up to something. Besides, that is, being members of my favorite rock band, Fluke."

"I've heard of Fluke," Chas said. "Aren't you 'The rock band with the big heart'?"

"That was before the shock absorbers on our van wore out," I said. "Now we're 'The rock band with the bad kidneys.'"

Chas laughed. "I've heard good things about your comedy, too."

"Thanks." I stuck out my hand. Chas offered a warm handshake that seemed to commit him to liking you.

Richard asked, "Any new songs tonight?"

"One," Bill said. "Dudley will give you the music." Dudley, our drummer, wrote most of our songs; songs that made you remember, with a chill, that great feeling of the first month of falling in love.

"Terrific." Richard moved behind the bar and motioned us to sit down.

I sat and held my breath. I had no idea how much Chas weighed, but I was surprised when he sat on a chair and the legs didn't snap.

Richard returned with two plates of pastries, slid one in front of us and headed backstage with the other. Chas offered Bill and me first choice. We shook our heads.

"You sure?" Chas stuffed one into his mouth. And it was gone. "They're great. Really light and flaky."

For ten minutes, Chas talked about the delights of pastries, pies, and pizzas, the way men at sea talk about women. He remembered people by what they liked to eat, cities by his favorite restaurants. He was a nice man who'd been places and eaten things. He tucked pastry number three into his mouth.

"Where'd you work before today?" I asked.

He swallowed. "Just got out of prison. Almost died there."

Bill's eyebrows shot up. "Died? How?"

"Boredom. Food was tasteless. All starches." He selected a bear claw and balanced it tenderly. "Funny, though. Now that I'm out of prison, starches are all I can afford. You have any idea what it's like, being an ex-con, having to go around begging people to hire you?"

"We're rock musicians," I said. "We know all about it."

Chas snorted, his colossal white dome bobbing.

Bill leaned forward. "So why were you in prison?"

Chas choked down the pastry and lowered his eyes to a stack of pamphlets on the table.

"What are those?"

Bill wasn't the type to let his question go unanswered, but I, having no desire to upset the enormous man, reached for the stack of pamphlets, grabbed the conversational ball and threw it the hell into center field.

"Just some information about organizations we encourage our audience to support."

Bill's mouth was still agape at the nerve of me hijacking the conversation. He wouldn't have looked more surprised had I stabbed him with a fork.

"That's a list of cosmetic companies who don't use animals to test their products anymore. And the ones that still do, like the Terrig and Laurel corporations."

"How do they test cosmetics on animals—put rouge and lipstick on a pig, take it to a bar, and see if anyone asks it to dance?" Chas paused, seemingly for a laugh.

While I might laugh at deathbed pranks, stuff found wadded up in napkins, or even old reruns of "Three's Company," animal testing is one of two subjects I don't find humor in. The other is my ex-wife.

"More than twenty million animals die every year in the U.S. to test products such as nail polish, floor wax, and drain cleaners." I opened a pamphlet and pushed it to Chas.

He started reading, then pointed to a name under the heading "Products Killing Animals."

"Hey, I used this shampoo for a while." He rubbed his large bald head. "That was the year my hair fell out. You think the animals they tested it on died of *embarrassment*?"

"They died from the incredible pain of having shampoo forced down their throats without anesthetics."

Chas blinked rapidly.

"The animals suffer convulsions and paralysis," I said, "and bleed from their eyes, nose, and mouth."

Chas looked as if he'd bitten into a Quarter-Pounder and found an ear.

"How'd you get into cosmetics and animals? How'd you even find out what goes on?"

I wasn't sure I should tell him. I tilted my empty glass to buy time. Why not, though. He was Richard's longtime friend . . .

My brother looked Chas square in the eye. I suspected he was readying to again press Chas about why he'd gone to prison. Bill began, "Why were you—"

"Eight years ago," I interrupted, and Bill's eyebrows went up like a drawbridge opening, probably because I had never interrupted him before, and he knew I'd been counting on this distinction to get me into heaven at a later date.

Chas's eyes gleamed bright with attention.

"My sister," I continued, "having no idea the cosmetic industry used animals for testing, took a summer job at Terrig Lab as a clinical technician. At first, it didn't look too bad. She trained dogs in the lab to run on a treadmill. Then she found out these dogs were bombarded with massive doses of radiation, and they ran only because electric shocks were applied. Shock intensity was increased until the dogs died. The experiment proved nothing but continued thanks to funding from our tax dollars. Corky was so sickened by the unnecessary cruelty that she got in touch with an organization that rescued animals."

"It must be my speech impediment," Chas said. "I try to ask how you got involved, and darned if I don't ask how your sister got involved by mistake. Let me give it another shot. How did you get involved?"

Bill began tapping his shoe against the leg of the table.

I cleared my throat. "The Animal Liberation Front asked Corky not to quit her job, they needed her on the inside. But Corky understood that if anything happened to the lab, as its newest employee she would be a suspect. So, the night of the liberation she invited three fellow technicians to her apartment for dinner."

When Chas nodded, I realized I was explaining the importance of an alibi to an ex-con.

"She was also worried about her lab key. What if the A.L.F. didn't return it before she had to go to work? Someone might guess she'd lent it out, which might make her a suspect, alibi or no alibi. So she asked me, as a favor, to handle the key. I was supposed to just open the lab door. A thirty-second involvement. But when I saw the team needed help, I followed them inside."

Seeing that scene in my mind, I closed my eyes.

When I opened them, Chas was waiting patiently.

"Tell me," he said softly.

"Thirty irradiated dogs lay inside a small corral. Some were partially dissected and still alive. The rest were dead. I helped carry the living dogs outside into a van. They decided to leave the dead dogs behind. When I was locking the lab door, movement drew me to the shadows and to what I was pretty sure was a dead English sheepdog. I went back inside and checked for a pulse. None.

"But I thought I heard crying. I stood motionless. Again, I sensed the sheepdog was moving. I rechecked his pulse. None. Then I noticed a small dog nobody had seen because his fur was just like the dead dog's he was snuggled against.

"I tried coaxing the live dog to go with me, but he wouldn't leave his friend. When I tried to move him, he bared his teeth and growled. Outside, the van's engine roared to life. I pleaded with the small dog to come with me. The headlights of the van flashed on. I lifted the dead sheepdog. 'Come on, fella,' I said, 'you're coming home with me.' I carried the dead dog outside, hoping the live dog would follow. I didn't know it then, but the live dog was blind from exposure to radiation. Navigating by smell and sound, he followed his friend and jumped into the van, where he rested his head on the body."

"Did he make it?" Chas asked.

"He could, in fact, bite your leg right now."

Chas slowly moved his eyes downward. My blind dog, Hoover, was asleep under the table. I scratched him behind the ears and he flapped his tail against the floor.

Hoover is a shaggy dog, the kind a child with a minimum knowledge of anatomy could draw, no details required—a shaggy dog that isn't a particular kind of shaggy dog. When I stopped scratching him, he put his head back down. I dropped a beer nut on the floor and Hoover vacuumed it up.

Chas watched Hoover a minute longer, then turned his

attention to the literature on the table.

"You stick this stuff on car windshields?"

"No. We put the pamphlets by the door, and drop the leaflets from a radio-controlled model helicopter we hover over the audience."

"Smokes, aren't those gizmos noisy?"

"Not with the new turbine engine technology."

"If you want me to, I'll hand out leaflets between flights."

"Thanks, but if we hand 'em out, people act put-upon. If we drop 'em from the air, people actually dive to snag them." I shrugged, failing in yet another attempt to understand human nature.

All at once the background noise died away. Richard peered from behind the jukebox holding a plug in one hand and waving an empty pastry plate with his other.

"On in ten!"

Like Pavlov's dog, my adrenaline began to flow.

Chas excused himself and stood. His chair sighed with relief.

With Hoover following us very closely, Bill and I followed the light of a red EXIT sign down the hall and turned left into the dressing room.

Illuminated by a single bulb, the dressing room was an all-purpose room where breaks were taken between sets and brooms and mops were stored. Scattered on the walls were posters featuring rock greats. Alice Cooper, Jim Morrison, and Janis Joplin were pale yellow, faded, and peeling.

Ann Berlin was relaxing on a folding chair and changing the reed in her saxophone. Tonight, instead of wearing the dark camouflage clothes she'd worn as an operative the previous night, her athletic body was graciously displayed in a sparkling green gown. I'd only ever seen her dressed in those two extremes, camouflaged or alluring, which made it hard for me to picture her as a lawyer.

James "Dudley" Mack, our drummer, was tapping a

rhythm with his fingers on an Igloo cooler and making Ann laugh. I used to envy Dudley for his social skills. He was everything I was too cautious to be: moody, emotional, full of rage, love and enthusiasm.

But I no longer envied him. Long ago I'd decided certain social skills were beyond me, and now I stood silently enjoying his lively banter, with no more comprehension of its creation than a sea gull staring at the space shuttle.

Yet, inside Dudley was a subtle sadness. With strong chiseled features, he was a living caricature of Dudley Do-Right, and actively pursued by women. But he hadn't dated anyone since graduating with a biology degree from the University of Massachusetts—at which time the only girl he'd ever loved, my sister Corky, broke up with him. Ever since that heartbreak, eight years ago, he'd avoided other women and spent his free time studying the behavior of ducks while volunteering at the Boston Aquarium.

Bill slid a trashcan aside with his foot and stepped in front of me.

"Be careful of what you say to Chas. He was doing a little digging, don't you think?"

"Don't worry," I said. "Any friend of a good man like Richard is probably a good man, too."

"You really believe that?"

I thought I did, until I said it out loud.

"You win."

While I was taking the compulsory eight-count, my brother was smiling benignly, leaning on a mop.

"Something isn't right about that guy," he said. "Know what I mean?"

"Sure do. He requested *Muskrat Love*."

"Go ahead, joke away." Bill fingered a broken mop handle, giving some evidence of intentions to reverse its direction and turn me into a Clark-kabob.

I gazed dolefully into the eyes of Janis Joplin.

A knock came on the dressing room door.

"On in two!"

Ann set down her saxophone and walked over to me. In a silky voice she said, "You're not limping. Your leg okay?"

"Much better, thanks." I stuffed a fistful of Cracker Jacks into my mouth.

"I wish you wouldn't eat those."

"Murrouph." I swallowed and held the box out to her. "Sorry. Did you want them? You could just say no, you don't have to make that kind of face at me."

Her fingers touched my hand. A whisper touch, there and gone.

"Haven't you eaten enough?"

I looked into the box and smiled at her. "No. The box isn't empty."

Again, someone pounded on the door. Hoover's ears thrust out to the sides in a way that seemed to signal both alarm and curiosity. He waddled toward the sound. I stepped over the trashcan and opened the door to my sister standing squarely in the door frame.

"What are you doing here?" I asked. There had to be a problem for her to leave the makeshift animal hospital, especially since it was getting late and tomorrow was a school day. Herding third graders took energy.

"I know you're about ready to go on," she said. "But when your set's over, meet me at the bar. I'll have a Cavalry Charger waiting for you."

That worried me. The last time I had a drink I ended up staggering around the room holding my head, screaming, "Get this thing off me." She knew that.

"I'll have one ready for you," she said, confirming my worries. Something was wrong.

The other band members filtered past us. Dudley stopped next to Corky.

"The adoption papers are ready. Just sign them and you can walk me home."

Corky continued looking at me, ignoring Dudley. If she

expected him to give up, though, she had badly underestimated him.

Dudley backed off toward the stage.

"I'm housebroken, had all my shots, and don't bark at night. Unless you want me to."

Dudley had teased Corky for so many years I wondered if she knew how much Dudley still loved her. Or if she felt love was perilous. Or if she simply was uncomfortable around someone whose natural enthusiasm had once propelled him out of a car to dance with a tollbooth attendant.

Bill handed me my guitar. I watched the departing backs of the other band members. I understood why Corky was keeping bad news from us until later. The first set established the tone of the evening.

She nodded at me, eyes wide, and drifted into the crowd.

I could guess the gist of her concern. A lot of planning was going into the liberation of rabbits from Laurel in six days. She'd probably hit a snag.

"Let's go." Hoover stood up, wagged his tail, and we scrambled onstage together. He took his spot on a throw rug that I put in the same place each night so he could find it.

I looked across the dance floor, past several rows of tables, to where Corky stood in front of the cartoon chef, rocklike in the river of people flowing past her. Although she was directly between the chef and his pot, he didn't seem to notice her.

Corky is attractive but she doesn't do much to enhance her appearance. Tonight, her long dark hair looked as if it had been yanked on for a week by her third-grade class, and her clothes didn't make a statement except a general one of disinterest. Dudley's obsession with her puzzled me. Was he interested in her solely because she was the only woman he couldn't have? And did she ignore him because she understood his obsession?

The lights came up and the crowd noise went down as if they were wired to the same switch. Onstage, Richard was highlighted by a single blue spotlight.

"Ladies and gentlemen, as you know, there are bands that aren't very good, there are bands that are pretty good, and every once in a while a band surfaces that is so good it transcends the very definition of rock 'n' roll. Ladies and gentlemen, I give you—a pretty good band."

A crack of applause split through the laughter as Richard took his place behind the bank of keyboards. The blue spotlight swung to Dudley, outlining his drums. As he kept a steady beat on the toms he leaned toward his mike.

"Heard the joke about the guy who goes to Africa? Gets off the plane and the first sound he hears is tribal drums. He turns to a native, 'What's with the drums?' The native says, 'Very bad if drums stop.' The guy gets to his hotel and the drums are still pounding. He asks the bellhop, 'What's with the drums?' The bellhop replies, 'Very bad if drums stop.' Later, he's walking through town when suddenly the drums stop. The guy turns to a lady near him and asks, 'Now what happens?' The lady says, 'Very bad. Now comes the bass solo.'"

The audience rocked with laughter.

Bill's bass guitar and the tribal rhythm of Dudley's drumsticks launched us into Raw Youth's "Tame Yourself."

If you are weaker, I will eat you
If you are smaller, I will defeat you
King of all I see
I will proudly wear your memory
What separates me from the wildest beast?
It is greed and vanity
And the bigger brain, oh the shame, the shame.

Bill and Richard traded leads. Staccato arpeggios burst out, ricocheted back and forth and into lightning riffs, like speeding bullets, making me feel as though I were caught in some sort of a crossfire.

When I looked to where Corky had been standing, there was only a man dancing, large enough to have consumed her whole, staring blankly into infinity, rotating his butt like he was stirring the cartoon lobster pot with it. As he stirred, something in my stomach seemed to slither and coil.

I no longer feared the passage of time. I was certain I'd stopped it while waiting for the set to end. When it finally did, Hoover and I rushed to the bar to wait for Corky. I spun onto a stool in front of Mervyn the bartender, and Hoover curled around the base of the stool.

Mervyn was as tiny and fragile as a sparrow. His sea-blue eyes took in his surroundings through wire-rimmed glasses that sat low on his nose. Although I knew nothing about his past, conversations with him revealed considerable expertise in the field of deviant psychology.

I nodded to Mervyn, who poured me a glass of water. I splashed the straw around and about in the icy water while scanning the crowd for Corky.

Seated three stools to my right was a man in a brown leather coat whose granite face seemed incapable of the flexibility required for a smile. Although his voice was soft as he talked to Mervyn, I caught enough of his words to realize he was asking about Fluke, and their rapidity gave the impression he wasn't just passing the time of day. I leaned toward him, trying to hear more.

The male conversations around me broke off—a sign Ann was approaching—but I was surprised when she swung onto the stool next to mine. My brain sounded an alert that it was shutting down. I've never developed whatever part of the brain it is that enables men to say whatever you're supposed to say to women. I suspect that even John Hinkley, who shot President Reagan to impress Jodie Foster, knows more about women than I do.

"How's it going, Clark?" Ann said.

"Fine." I scooped a handful of beer nuts from the bowl on the counter.

"Where's Corky?"

"Don't know, she disappeared."

"Ah. A rather unusual usage of the word 'fine' of which I wasn't aware."

Mervyn came down and wiped up some of the liquid off the counter in front of me.

"What'll it be?"

"A Cavalry Charger, please." Rarely do I drink, for fear of saying something stupid, but it seemed a little late to be having qualms.

"Make it two," Ann said.

Mervyn made us two Cavalry Chargers using half the bottles on the back bar. Our drinks came and we sipped them while we looked for Corky.

"Clark," Ann said. "Can I ask you something?"

I cocked my head to listen.

"I've known your sister more than a year and I still haven't figured out why she gets so tense whenever Dudley's around?"

I pondered Ann's question as we both watched two men wander in who looked as if they'd cheerfully disembowel their own grandmothers for the price of a beer. Their presence gave me a measure of joy; not because I approved of this eccentricity in customers, but because their patronage meant we were drawing some of the crowd from the Stagger Back Inn, the topless bar across the street.

For several years the Stagger Back had steadily lost business to the Lobster. A few months ago, they closed for two weeks. When they reopened, Bill and I crossed Rosy Street to see what had changed. The doorman looked down at us from the unfathomable heights of his exalted position. I suspected the owner had stationed him at the door and told him that any customer was a bum until he proved himself otherwise. Showed him what he meant by proof, then put it back into the cash register.

Inside, a stagnant mysterious smoke clung to the few molecules of oxygen I gasped for. The lumpy shape of cigarettes suggested most of the crowd rolled their own. It was the kind of place you hoped you wouldn't meet your sister.

Bill and I sat at a table near the bar. Topless waitresses hustled around, making me nervous. Ten minutes later, a band came onstage but no one seemed to listen. People came into the bar, looked around and left.

When we decided to leave, I made a theatrical show of feeling for my wallet and being relieved to find it still in my pocket.

"I really should carry traveler's checks in a place like this."

Although I had soaked in the dank atmosphere of the Stagger Back Inn only a few minutes, I recognized its patrons when they came into the Lobster and began to breath normally again. The two new ones took a seat.

"When Corky broke up with Dudley," I said, "she insisted she was a jinx on him because he almost electrocuted himself the day they decided to go steady."

Ann gave me a sidelong glance.

"Then I understand why the issue isn't resolved for Dudley. He knows Corky is too sensible to believe in jinxes."

"True. But I still don't know her real reason. Although . . ." I let myself trail off, thinking that ever since Dad died,

Corky had seemed afraid of getting close to anyone. Or was I just projecting? I bombed in another beer nut.

Without a fair and adequate warning, Ann asked, "So, what went wrong with your marriage?"

I swallowed the beer nut the wrong way and nearly choked, making it too late to work a mystified smile onto my face that might convey I hadn't the slightest idea what she was talking about. So I forged ahead, even though my brain was twinkling with warning lights like the console of a crashing airliner.

"Didn't need a wife, I had a television set to insult my intelligence."

I crossed my legs, toyed with the button on my shirt pocket, then rattled the ice cubes in my glass to see if any liquid was trapped beneath them. Mervyn answered the rattle. With his keen sense of deviant behavior, he saw I was in trouble and mixed me another Charger.

A few gulps of my second drink led me into my past.

"Six years ago, after I graduated from college, I got married. Seems a lifetime ago."

But how many lifetimes must pass before I can forget that gut-wrenching moment when Jessie told me she wanted a divorce. Jesus. I can't believe it still hurts to think about it. I don't think I can talk about it.

So I lied. "My wife was always mad at me."

"About what?"

I put my glass down and twisted it against my soggy napkin.

"She said I never listened to her. Or something like that."

Ann didn't return my feeble attempt at a smile.

"There's not much else to tell," I said. "Our marriage didn't last long. Although it did teach me one valuable lesson. If a woman says, 'We need to talk,' you should treat it like a hotel fire: don't breathe, stay low to the ground, and crawl rapidly for the nearest exit."

I could tell by the look on Ann's face that something was

wrong, and that it had to do with what I'd said.

"Clark?" She looked me over thoroughly, perhaps measuring me for a straitjacket. "You go to an awful lot of trouble to appear, even to your closest friends, like you have no feelings. You offer no more depth than . . . than the goofy sayings on these cocktail napkins!" She picked up a wet napkin, let it drain a little, then flopped it gently across my nose. "How come?"

"But the napkins are very funny." I let the wet one stay where it was.

"Funny," she conceded, "but not very deep."

I felt I ought to say something—I'm sorry I'm alive, or something..

"Women are naturally deeper than men," I said. "You should have seen me when I found out I wasn't ever going to be a woman. I cried like a baby. Hell of a thing to tell a kid." I offered Ann my warmest, most charming smile.

"What the devil are you smirking at?" Her green eyes looked hurt and clouded in the brief moment I saw them before she glanced off into space, ignoring me. *Yep, another minute and she'll be curled up in my lap.* I took the wet napkin off my nose.

Mervyn materialized, pushing his wire-rimmed glasses back into place, offering me more beer nuts. I said thank you, then tried not to look at them. One bowl was enough.

Ann looked back at me. "I don't know if you realize it, but your wife has left scars on you that aren't properly healing. Why?"

Opening and closing my mouth, I was unable to bring myself to offer an answer that wasn't as good as the question. I gazed out the window instead.

"Is it still snowing outside?"

Ann didn't answer. The noise of the bar flooded in on me. The rest of the band had disappeared.

"We're due backstage."

* * *

Corky didn't show up during the second break, either. I figured there must have been some emergency and she'd left in a hurry. After the third set, Bill told us all that he was headed for the men's room.

I caught his arm. "That guy over there with the granite face looks familiar. Could he be a local reporter?"

"Could be," Bill said. But, then again, he was on his way to the men's room. I suspect he would have agreed if I'd said God is a woodchuck.

Hoover followed Ann backstage, his rear end waddling busily. Dudley walked past me toward the bar, and I joined him, heading for a booth reserved for band members.

To our chagrin, the booth was inhabited by Cavalry's three most ubiquitous convicted felons. Their leader, Lester Gillis, was a short man. Maybe five-two, but stocky, swarthy, with a large mustache. A soul less charitable than myself would have said he looked like an organ grinder who'd just stomped his monkey to death. He was leaning back in a silver fox fur coat, watching Dudley and me approach as though we were maggots climbing onto a wedding cake.

A purplish tattoo, scratched into the knuckles of the right hand of the tallest felon, said Mungo.

I recognized the third, a rodent-faced man, from newspaper photos. He had a shaved head and a nose that looked sewn back on. His name was Harry "The Rat" Hickabob. His arms were folded across his barrel chest, and he'd eaten half the RESERVED sign to educate the waitresses.

"Excuse me, gentlemen," Dudley said softly. "This booth is reserved for Fluke."

The Rat said clearly that he didn't much care. I understood it even without the gesture.

Mungo stood up, and up. Towering over us, he looked down, his eyes red with alcohol, showing all the humanity of rusted ball bearings.

"Why'd ya steal our customers from the Stagger Back?"

Rather than answer I tried to figure out if these guys

presence and Corky's absence might be in some way connected.

I forced my attention back onto Mungo, who was lecturing on the high cost of dental work and the difficulty of a musician trying to earn a living with two broken arms. As he finished he looked down at me and shifted his gaze to a small black ant crossing the piebald floor. He crushed the ant, grinding it as though it were a giant tarantula.

"I hate bugs." He was looking at me.

"It was only an—"

Crack! The Rat smashed an empty beer bottle over the edge of the wooden table. Glass sprayed. Dozens of glistening wet shards stuck to my cotton jacket.

Everyone in the bar was watching and pretending they weren't; their stillness gave them away.

The Rat pointed the sharp edge of the bottle at me.

"You ain't listening. It's pissin' us off. . . ."

My first instinct was to take away the broken bottle and feed it to him. But there was no way to tell to what extent he was bluffing, or to what extent he was insane.

Dudley leaned toward me and whispered, "Get Richard."

I backstepped. It didn't go unnoticed.

"Hey, Baby Face," The Rat hollered. "A squirrel ever run up your pants leg and down the other—disappointed?" Mungo threw back his head and let out a great peal of gleeful laughter.

I was so preoccupied backing away that I didn't get around to feeling insulted until much later. After a few more steps, I turned and hightailed it for Richard. It took a concerted effort not to look back to see if anyone was following me, as I had no desire to be skewered on the business end of a broken beer bottle. I wove my way through the crowd to where Richard was polishing glasses behind the bar.

I plopped onto a stool in front of him, as I'd done countless times in the months following my mother's death. After the rest of the band had gone home, with nowhere to go, I'd sit and talk with him about nothing in particular. He didn't seem to mind. It was in keeping with his personality to listen and to laugh, amused by the world and dead serious at the same time. With caring eyes that seemed to be just one step ahead, he'd anticipate what I'd say, yet never seem bored.

Richard stopped polishing a beer glass, hung it upside down in a glass cabinet, folded his towel, and then walked toward the booth.

Mungo and The Rat were still laughing. Dudley was waiting, but Lester, like my sister, had disappeared.

Richard slid into the booth and put his arm around Mungo. Mungo grinned broadly, as if the canary had just landed in the cat bowl.

"Where did Mr. Gillis go?" Richard asked. "And to what do we owe the pleasure of your company tonight?"

"You wanna know why *we're* here?" Mungo said. "Well, I wanna know why *anyone's* here? They should be across the street listening to the Four Maldehydes."

The night Bill and I visited the Stagger Back Inn, it seemed to us that if the Four Maldehydes didn't go out of business it would be only because nobody noticed they were ever *in* business. They were ignored despite strutting around wearing white leather Pampers over black Spandex tights and snarling at the audience. One Maldehyde had painted a slit on his throat with musical notes dripping down like blood. Another tried to eat his microphone.

Mungo's laugh, too loud for indoor use, finally died. He wriggled his fingers at Petey, a pleasant waitress who'd worked at the Lobster over ten years and was confused in demeanor except when waitressing. Petey hesitated, then saw Richard and started over. When she reached the table, marinating in perfume that smelled like fruit salad, she said,

174

"Hi, Mungo. May I help you?"

Petey knows Mungo?

"Sure, babe, you can help me. Tell me why your phone's always busy."

Petey lifted her chin. "After my first date with you, I took my phone off the hook."

"It's been over a month."

"Small price to pay."

Mungo glared at her. "You can't talk to customers like that!"

"You're right." Petey tossed her hair. "Sorry. Can I get you anything? Beer? Wine? Rabies shot?"

Mungo all but came out of his seat. "Scotch. No tap water in it this time." He blew her a big sloppy kiss, stuck out his tongue and wiggled it. "Stick it where I *remember* how much you *like* it, bitch." He cupped his hands in front of his chest and moved them back and forth. I assumed he was not indicating Petey had an arthritic condition.

Even in the darkened bar, Petey's blush was visible. Mungo and The Rat howled and gave every impression that these were the moments they lived for.

Richard made a fist and told Petey to skip the drink. He looked at Mungo and held one thumb up in an exaggerated version of an umpire's "you're out!" sign.

Mungo leaned back in casual defiance.

Richard nodded towards the kitchen. Chas Blat was rounding the corner, his massive bulk jiggling in remembrance of calories past. Chas's white marble scars, aglow under the fluorescent lighting, made the scars of Frankenstein's monster look like cosmetic surgery.

The Rat, about to slurp another swig of beer, dropped the bottle as if it had been shot out of his hand.

"When did he get out of prison?"

"Do you expect to be moving along now," Richard said, "or would you both like to wake up with your asses sewn to your faces?"

"If your goon touches me," The Rat said, "I'll take you to

court and take *every cent* you have."

Richard laughed. "You can reach into my pockets and do that."

The Rat blinked rapidly. Twice. As if sand had blown in his face. "Then," he said in a voice too shaky to have conviction, "then I'll call the police."

Richard leaned forward. "If there is anything you'd like to tell the police, I suggest you jot it down now, *before* Chas hits you."

Chas was fifteen feet away and closing. Mungo and The Rat vacated the booth in all haste.

* * *

As the fourth set started, Lester swaggered across the dance floor with his fox fur coat draped over his arm. Where had he been? My anxiety returned about Corky.

Since the mood of the crowd grew increasingly somber as the evening wore on, much of our fourth set was blues. Richard played melodies that sounded like somebody crying. Ann interlaced them with slow, sad sax riffs, and Bill picked his bass, wincing as though tearing each note from his chest.

Near the end of the set, Ann drifted across the stage. Her effect on men in the audience was unanimous: heads moved in a synchronized turn that would've made a chorus line proud.

"Let me introduce the band," she said low into the mike. "On keyboards, the owner of the Lobster—Richard Tipton."

Richard jumped into his B. B. King-gone-mad finale, tearing through blues riffs on three banks of synths. The crowd cheered.

"On drums—Dudley Mack."

Dudley began his solo, playing the snare slightly ahead of the bass drum for a driving beat. He twirled his sticks in the air and: BOMP chaka chaka chaka BOMP!

"On bass guitar—Bill Baker."

My brother stepped into the spotlight, his mane of golden hair rippling as he jammed into a viciously crisp bass solo.

"Rhythm guitar—Clark Baker."

While Bill flew the Cobra, raining leaflets over the

audience, I improvised. As I hit my final lick, Bill deftly landed the Cobra at my feet.

I went to the microphone and introduced Ann. She stepped forward and started a melody. As she played, a murmur swept through the room in a rising wave. Moving toward the stage was a beefy, purple-haired young man, his face blood-red with anger. Behind Purple Hair, pushing him forward, were two equally angry young men. Crumpled in Purple Hair's right fist were the pamphlets I'd put by the door. As he pushed forward, the crowd parted in front of him, their voices stilled in anticipation of trouble. *This must have been what Corky wanted to warn us about.*

When Purple Hair reached the stage, Bill went over to meet him—to push him back from the stage, I thought, but instead he helped him climb up. As Purple Hair brushed past me, one of the buttons on his jacket snagged my guitar strings and made a sound not unlike a chicken caught in a vacuum cleaner. He grabbed my mike from its stand.

"The Bible tells us in Genesis 1:27 that God created man in His image!" Purple Hair proceeded to "shame" the audience with a rousing sermon that imitated budget television evangelism, getting boos and applause in equally frenzied parts.

"Psalms 8:6 tells us man has dominion over all other things. And in Hebrews 7:25, God told people to sacrifice animals for their sins."

Animal-rights supporters, about half the audience, howled their protest. Applause burst from a dozen or so other people.

Purple Hair shredded pamphlet after pamphlet, tossing the scraps high into the air, where they drifted down like confetti. As he preached and tore pamphlets, the applause grew as if the crowd thought turning against the band was part of the evening's entertainment. A steadily growing number targeted us with beer nuts, napkin holders, the baby Jesus from the nativity scene, and a leather Army boot. Within moments the Lobster looked like a terrorist training camp.

A fight broke out in front of Bill and me. Hoover retreated, bumping blindly into a speaker before threading his way between two amps.

There was some poetry in the melee: one man was thrown clear across the room, spinning and staggering and flailing with his arms, while three men dove swanlike out of the way.

Chas came striding around the corner, his heavy head moving like a wrecker's ball. When Purple Hair saw him, he vaulted down from center stage. Too late. Chas collared him, then dragged him wrenching and squirming toward the door.

The crowd kept pressing in on us.

Dudley jumped up from his stool, tapped loudly on his boom mike, and pointed at Purple Hair. "There, ladies and gentlemen, goes the president of Fluke's fan club." Most of the crowd turned to look. Some laughed. The intervals between the sounds of bottles and glasses exploding around us lengthened, like popcorn almost finished popping. "Our Pres just wants to keep us from getting too big for our britches. He's afraid if we get famous, he'll get famous too, and someone will publish those *nude* photos of him." Dudley laughed his infectious laugh and the crowd laughed, shattering the hostility of the moment.

Before the crowd could work its fury back up, Richard spread timbres across octaves, building an enormous layered crescendo. Instead of pressing forward, the crowd swayed with the music, back and forth, like sea plants at the bottom of the ocean.

* * *

Backstage, Dudley took two dripping cans of Diet Coke from the bed of ice in the cooler and tossed one underhanded to Bill.

"Thanks."

"You're welcome. Now I'm going to kill you." Dudley formed a gun with his hand and pantomimed blowing Bill away. "What were you thinking when you helped that kid up onto the stage?"

"Hey. I'm awfully sorry." Bill broke off the pop-top and poised it in midair, like a knife. "Here, I'll slash my wrists."

"Let me say this as politely as I can. What diseased germ invaded your brain?" Dudley began rubbing his right temple with his fingertips.

"What's the rude version, you kick me as you say it?"

"Listen, just try to remember that people who interrupt our gigs with our pamphlets *crumpled* probably aren't looking for autographs."

Bill threw the pop-top into the trashcan as if it were something he should have done yesterday.

"It doesn't matter what that kid said tonight. He's been a regular fan; you should've recognized him. You're not thinking straight because Corky showed up."

Cheap shot. Had I been refereeing this argument instead of sitting in the stands, I'd have blown a whistle, flag on the play. I looked down at Hoover, who had his mouth clamped shut, a sign of worry. He worries when his people seem upset.

Dudley groaned. "You're weirder than the things I get free with my breakfast cereal."

Bill walked away. Dudley, not finished talking, began speaking to a quart-size food blender balanced on an overturned metal pail next to the doorway.

"Bill's barking mad." Dudley was leaning over, eye-to-multifaceted-eye with a tarantula, Smuffkins. Smuffy was my pet and she traveled everywhere with us. Her traveling home, a broken fourteen-speed food processor, had a sign below the power switch: AND YOU THINK THERE'S STRESS IN *YOUR* LIFE.

"Don't take it personally," I answered for Smuffy. "It's been a rough month for us all and Bill's high-strung anyway. We ought to be sympathetic."

"It's just that sometimes his attitude . . ."

"I know."

Despite being a man who rarely did anything unkind, Bill gave the impression of being capable of any enormity. His mind was always going a mile a minute and when he started talking he sounded like a clock with a spring wound too tight— at any moment he might start ringing frantically and hop off the shelf.

Dudley winked at Smuffy. "He needs an analyst or a psychiatrist or a good spanking, which I'm about to give him."

Corky burst in. "Clark—" Seeing Dudley, she stopped short.

Dudley grinned. "How's our baby?"

Corky considered him quizzically.

"Oh no—" Dudley said. "I'm sorry, it wasn't you."

"If I have a baby, somebody had better tell Jesus he has a little brother."

Corky, like me, uses humor as a shield. Unlike our own brother, Dudley accepts this fact.

Bill still hopes Corky and I will one day drop our shields and get in touch with our humanness, become complete human beings. To this effect, he suggests we study the Bible.

I stopped believing in God when I read that He told man that he could sacrifice animals for his use. It seemed to me that anybody so insensitive to other species could be only a human being in disguise.

I explained to Bill my theory that man invented God to justify his own self-obsession as a species, his unfounded claim that he is of more value than other creatures. Bill said my having such a theory was sure proof that Satan had sent a demon to infest my soul.

"You were right about trouble," I told Corky. "How'd you know about that kid?"

She shook her head. "I didn't."

"You didn't . . . why didn't you wait for me at the bar?"

"The father of one of my students recognized me and asked me to dance. Nice guy, but drunk. Out of character. So I excused myself and went to the pay phone to call A.L.F. members and warn them."

"About what?"

"Trouble. Remember the last van that pulled away from the Terrig Lab? Kristin told the driver to leave without her, that someone else was going to pick her up. She smuggled in a can of gasoline and, after everyone else was gone, turned off the fire alarms and set fire to the equipment."

Good for Kristin, taking initiative like that. Now Terrig couldn't simply replace the dogs.

"Who picked her up?"

Corky pushed away her hair, revealing a tear. "Nobody, Clark. That's what I'm trying to tell you . . . Kristin died in the fire."

My intestines lurched. I slammed my fist into Alice Cooper's face and cracked the wall-plaster underneath.

"Damn that Terrig. He taunted the protesters!"

"I talked with Kristin's mother, told her I was a friend of Kristin's and how sorry I was." Corky's voice was getting hoarse. "Her father grabbed the phone and started pumping me for information about the animal-rights cult that had brainwashed his daughter."

I was staring at the floor, hardly hearing her.

"Kristin's father—Clark?—Kristin's father might use his clout to get back at animal-rights organizations."

"Clout?"

"Her father is Beezil Terrig."

I slid down the wall and sat on the floor. I don't know why I was surprised she'd set fire to her own father's lab— a lot of people become animal-rights activists precisely because they *know* what goes on behind lab doors. Like Corky and me.

I shivered. I noticed my jacket was open and snapped it shut. I wasn't surprised when that didn't stop my shivering.

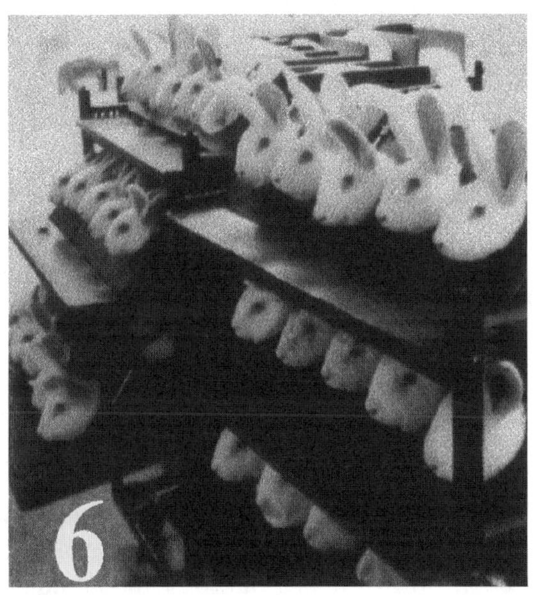

"On in ten."

I was sitting on the stage, immersed in sad thoughts, and watching the crowd's Brownian movement. Bill hustled up, stood close to me, but kept raking his eyes over the crowd.

"Somebody's going to kill Richard tonight."

"Beezil Terrig?"

"Don't know. I heard it on the soundcheck system." That didn't help much. We had six wireless microphones placed around the lounge to help us balance sound levels.

"Which channel?"

"Couldn't tell. When I looked over, it was scanning again."

"Recognize the voice?"

"Cold. It would fit the guy with the granite face. Second row."

Following Bill's eyes, I saw Granite nervously twisting his shoulders, as if something were crawling down his back.

I could warn Richard, but Bill was probably wrong. He was pessimistic; while some people saw the glass as half full, he saw it as empty and cracked.

"What should we do?" I said.

"If we play our wireless guitars, we can stay between Richard and Granite. But the voice I heard was talking to someone else. Watch for anyone pointing any—"

Bill's eyes had locked onto something moving behind me. I turned.

Dudley always moved like a dancer, smoothly, as though he heard music.

"Stay loose," he said. "Although our performance hasn't been one for the books, at least it's a concert and not a political rally, a soccer game, or a seminar on aluminum siding. And we still can hit our stride in the last set."

Dudley assumed we were suffering from our usual state of mind before going on, performance anxiety, which he never fully understood because he had talent. I suspect he could get some sort of music out of a ripe kumquat, even if he'd never played one before.

He patted our shoulders. "On in one."

Bill and I trailed close behind him, like baby ducks, to the dressing room, where we caught Ann eating Cracker Jacks. With a guilty expression she closed the box.

Richard came in and looked at his watch.

"Let's go."

He was so eager to lead us onstage that, although he ordinarily stepped aside for everybody, this time he commandeered a charge through the stage wings. Bill marched next to him, unnaturally close. I lagged behind to give Hoover a drink of water. If there was danger, I didn't want him onstage.

"Stay."

Hoover went rigid, arching his back and thrusting his head down and forward. I closed the door, inhaled deeply to calm myself, cut between two telephone-booth-sized amplifiers, and, not counting the cymbals I bumped into, slipped silently to my microphone.

I ran through my checklist: *Synthesizers on?* Check.

Amplifiers on? Check. *Escape route visible?* Check. All was in order.

The curtains opened and a rush of warm air from the lounge carried the smell of damp woolen coats. While I adjusted the height of my microphone, Bill, standing to my right, inched his mike forward, parallel with mine, so we could communicate with head nods.

I grabbed my guitar off its stand and strapped it on. A snappy up-tempo brush pattern kicked off the song "Slaves" by Fetchin' Bones. Gripping my pick, I stabbed nervously at the strings. Now and then I hit one.

Slaves of the twentieth century
Of science, fashion, industry, and gourmet
Lab cats, lab rats, in pain they squeal
What do you think a monkey feels
When his brain is split by cold hard steel?
No tears shampoo, so gentle and kind
A million rabbits, each one blind.
Who draws the line
Between slaves and you and me?

Richard moved around the stage, playing different keyboards, changing MIDI settings, adjusting amplifiers. Granite paced around the lounge, from the bar to his table to the men's room, and back, the angle between him and Richard continually changing. Trying to stay between them, Bill and I shuffled around and kept bumping into each other. Twice, when Granite reached into his pockets, Bill and I leapt to occupy the exact same spot. This is not easily accomplished, not in this physical universe, but we almost made it.

Finally, Ann tapped her microphone, signaling the last song of the set.

"On bass—Bill Baker."

Bill, concentrating on staying between Richard and Granite, played in a spacey, faraway style that Van Gogh might have arranged if he'd poked out his eye instead of dicing off his ear. Bill's was a brief solo, or so it seemed to me. I was next. If Granite was planning to kill Richard tonight he'd have to make his move soon.

Usually when I play my solo I stand in one spot. This time I had to move in front of Richard. After my introduction, I stepped to the front of the stage, leaped three feet in the air and came down in an unchecked split, pulling screaming harmonics off the top of the guitar neck to mask my own screams of pain. Then I rose in front of Richard, twirling and wailing. Really wailing.

After I finished my solo, I stepped gingerly past Ann as she came forward to her microphone.

"On keyboards, the owner of the Lobster, Richard Tipton."

I jerked my head around to fix Richard's location. *Oh no—* he'd strapped on his *portable* keyboard. With a smooth stride he stepped all the way to the front of the stage, saying as he passed me that he accepted the challenge.

Bill turned to me, blue eyes large. We both kept playing, but the sentiment "Oh, shit" came clearly through our guitars.

Richard laid a trumpet across his sound-sampling keyboard, overlaid a distorted guitar, and when he improvised fragments of random melody with his fingers, out came a riff that sounded like Miles Davis playing Jimi Hendrix.

Granite watched us with a bovine passivity. Maybe he was planning the attack for later, outside. Or maybe he was the wrong guy.

When Richard finished, Ann glided to the front of the stage.

"Thank you for coming to see us, and—" she held up the Army boot that had landed onstage "—thank you for all the lovely gifts. You've been a great audience." She looked at me.

"Remember," I said, "when you eat meat, there's more love in your belly than in your heart."

"On your way out," Ann said, brandishing scraps of paper, "Please take our pamphlet."

Bill waved. "Godspeed." The crowd started to disperse.

"If you support animal-rights," Dudley smiled, "I hope you'll get all your friends involved. If you don't support animal-rights, I hope you don't *have* any friends."

The jukebox blared back on. Richard headed for his office. Chas, running his finger over the scar on his cheek, followed right behind Richard.

As the bar emptied, I caught glimpses of Granite sitting at a table, drinking, watching the crowd as though he were looking for someone. I began untangling cables, one eye on him. At certain angles the dim lighting illuminated his face such that I felt I knew him—and the context in which I knew him was disturbing.

He lifted his glass and, as if unwilling to admit it was empty, turned it upward until he was looking through the bottom of it like a telescope. Then he put it down, stood, bundled himself in his coat, and walked away without leaving a tip.

Bill popped up in front of me.

"I'll stick with Richard. You follow Granite."

Granite was walking behind one of the last couples to leave, a charming blue-haired duo, wearing matching T-shirts decorated with razor blades. As Granite neared the exit, Ann was heading in my direction.

"I'm on the case." I slipped down from the stage.

Ann angled in front of me, her hand cupping the ends of her hair and squeezing as if testing its springiness.

"Want to get something to eat. . . ."

"Yes, uh." I stepped around her. "Be right back."

Granite was outside now. I stopped just inside the door, near the pillaged nativity scene, and peered out at the parking lot. When I pushed the door open a wet blast of snow hit me in the face like a slap. Turning away, I found myself nose to nose with Ann.

I looked back at the parking lot and Ann looked with me, her head beneath my head like a totem pole.

Granite stopped beside a fancy wine-colored car, reached

into his coat pocket, and pulled out a cell phone. Ann started to say something. I put my finger to my lips.

Granite faced us, hunched over, shielding the phone's mouthpiece from the wind. I couldn't hear what he was saying. Nor could I move closer—no cover, our van was the only other vehicle in the parking lot.

I strained to hear. For a split second the wind died, and I clearly heard Granite say, "Fluke is finished. History."

Ann was right behind me as I charged across the parking lot, leaning forward into the wind that was slowing as well as silencing our attack.

I hit Granite with a flying tackle. We slid over the icy pavement and into the rear tires of his car. My forehead bounced off the Y in the words GOODYEAR DOUBLE EAGLE. We both scrambled to our feet. Backing away from him, I stayed on my toes. As I moved, I measured Granite as I'd measured dozens of wrestling opponents. He seemed sluggish and my confidence duly built—until he *threw a punch.*

We spent a while trying to hit each other. I favored one particular uppercut that never seemed to make contact with anything but air. He, on the other hand, threw some pretty snappy boxing combinations. When he jabbed with his left, I backed away on tiptoe to his right. When he swung with his right, I danced to his left. While I dazzled him with my footwork, he blinded me with his punches.

Gaining confidence, he closed in, and accidentally stepped into one of my wild uppercuts. He doubled up and moaned. I held up my hand and stared at my knuckles, now pulsing with pain.

Ann jumped on Granite's back. He reached around, trying to pull her off, spinning first one way, then twisting the other, like a dog chasing his tail.

He finally stumbled. Before he regained balance, I wrestled him to the ground and pinned him facedown with his arms behind his back.

Ann sat down on his legs. "What did he do to deserve

this?"

"Didn't tip the waitress."

"Not funny," Granite said.

"Everyone's a critic. Did Terrig hire you? Why have you been following Fluke?"

When he didn't answer, I tried to reach into his trouser pockets to find a wallet. He bucked and nearly threw me off.

I leaned on him harder. "Where have I seen you before?"

"Er . . . how would I know?"

"Guess, or I'll keep sitting here, being funny, until you plead for mercy."

His eyes darted to a black object in the snow, then darted away. "That's better. See what happens when people communicate?" While straight-arming his head, I leaned over him, fished his cell phone out of the snow, and found my friend, the redial button.

I'd learned a trick while married. Whenever I found my wife gone, I'd tap the redial button to determine if she'd been talking to her friends, as she'd claimed, or to someone I hadn't met. Before long I recognized a pattern. She lied when her calls had gone to a lawyer's office. But, although I knew where she was going, I never imagined the reason.

I pushed RECALL, SEND, then waited. Two rings, then a pick-up.

"Hello?"

"Who's this?"

"Who you looking for?"

"You. We've captured your accomplice."

He hung up. I poked Granite's shoulder.

"Your partner coming?"

Granite didn't answer. I tossed the phone into the nearest snow bank. With a renewed burst of energy he twisted and struggled. Evidently I'd needed to violate his personal property to convince him that I meant business.

"Why do you want to kill Richard?"

"Kill somebody? You're crazy!" He twisted violently, rocking me. I saw Bill standing in the entranceway of the Lobster and suddenly remembered his words: the threat to kill Richard had come from someone with a cold voice. Granite's voice was deep and warm. I had the wrong guy.

Bill, yet unaware I was sitting on perhaps a completely innocent pillar of the community, slid up to us with a little snicker in his eye. Wanting him to hear Granite's voice, hoping I was wrong, I asked Granite: "Where's your accomplice?"

His answer was drowned by a nerve shattering "Phooooommmmm" from the Howling Lobster.

Ann and I used Granite as a launch pad and rocketed past my stunned brother toward the noise. Its dying echo included splintering wood and cracking glass, followed by shouting from Richard's office.

Richard's office was a long, rectangular room with high wooden rafters. Its Spartan furnishings consisted of a desk, a filing cabinet, a green plastic couch, animal-rights posters on the walls, and a rubber tree. At the base of the tree Chas was kneeling over Richard, on his back in a pool of blood. Richard's face was riddled with small scarlet spots, his white shirt soaked in red.

I felt my heart in my chest as if it had just started pumping the moment before.

The wall behind Richard was splintered around knee-high, and blood was splattered over the words on the poster: "I am in favor of animal rights as well as human rights. This is the way of a whole human being—Abraham Lincoln."

Dudley ran in. "Oh God! I'll call an ambulance!"

I sank to my knees beside Richard and put my ear to his face. He was breathing. At that moment, it was enough.

Each breath he took seemed as if it might be his last, but after a grueling pause there would be another. Scarcely breathing myself, I pressed his shirt against his stomach, trying to stop the blood. He felt cold to the touch. Nausea rose in my throat and I swallowed hard to push it back down. My knees were wet with blood. Chas was motionless, tears pouring from his eyes.

I used a cushion from the couch to raise Richard's hips; the bleeding slowed. I pulled the cover from the couch and spread it over him. I didn't know what else to do.

Somewhere a siren wailed. Like a wolf answering a mating call, another joined in. Ann knelt beside us and took Richard's hand. I struggled to my feet and went outside.

An ambulance slid to a halt in front of the Lobster and three paramedics jumped out. I led them to the office, then went back outside when I heard more sirens. Three patrol cars careened up, their lights casting electric red ribbons on the snowy pavement and across the faces of the gathering gawkers.

Two officers cordoned off the sidewalk, one stayed to hold back the expanding crowd, others swarmed the area, digging around, flashlights slicing into the darkness around the building. Police radios buzzed and chattered in the background.

As the crowd pushed forward, I retreated to the spot where I'd tackled Granite. Although he was gone, hiding deep in my mind was a clue to his identity.

The paramedics carried Richard on a stretcher into the ambulance. I saw his face, eyes closed. I tried to find words to express my feelings and settled for the most primitive.

"Noooo!"

Ann came over and put her arms around me. She looked up at me. Her eyes were shimmering with unspilled tears.

"He never hurt a fly," I said. *I even watched him help one once.*

* * *

I dropped the rest of the band at the hospital's emergency-room entrance, parked, and told Hoover to stay in the van. He knew every nuance of my voice and backed away from the door immediately.

Above the reception desk, metallic letters said "Paul Revere County Hospital." Thirty miles from home, this was where my father had begun his one-way trip to the final mystery beyond the grave.

The receptionist looked at me, "My goodness, those are dreadful bruises on your face. Come here."

I obeyed. Then I told her what I wanted and she directed me to the third floor.

The familiar brain-numbing smell of hospital disinfectant pervaded the waiting room. Bill and Ann stood rigidly against the far wall. Dudley was slumped in a chair.

"How is he?" I asked. Ann's freckled face, remarkably rich and intriguing, remained blank. I asked again, more softly. Her eyes sideswiped me. It wasn't the answer I wanted.

Twenty minutes later three policemen arrived and separated us. My cop led me to an empty room and took off his jacket. His arms were a lot bigger than Hulk Hogan's but without any muscle tone whatsoever—they might not have even had bones. He pulled out a notebook and asked me what I knew. I told him about Granite, and the death threat that Bill had overheard.

The cop feverishly scribbled notes and circled the words *death threat*. "That makes sense. I know people in Cavalry who hate Fluke even being here."

Our mere presence? It made me feel like a cat turd at a dog show.

"You're trying to cripple our town's biggest industry. You don't have a family to support, do you?"

"Aren't you glad?"

"Don't get smart with me."

That'd be a waste of time. I looked at my shoes before he could call for thumbscrews.

"Did you argue with Mr. Tipton, maybe over your percentage of the gate?" His eyes widened in accusation.

I met his eyes without flinching, but was too startled to respond.

"No need to answer. Fluke is somewhere near the center of this crime, and we intend to solve it."

As he grilled me, rephrasing the same questions, I started getting one of those dull headaches like the ones that squeeze behind my eyes whenever I think of my ex-wife. My answers didn't change, and he closed his notepad and left.

When I got back to the waiting room the others were already there, their interviews over.

"They tell you anything?" Ann asked me.

"Only that they've narrowed down the suspects to anyone in Fluke."

"I got the same spiel. It's typical. In law school my boyfriend studied cases like this." This was Ann talking. It was so rare she spoke of her past that Bill and Dudley looked twice to make sure of where the sound was coming from. "When a town wants a lynching, sometimes the law gets stretched before a neck does."

An intern rushed past. I suddenly stopped worrying about anything but Richard. I plopped down next to Bill and quietly waited.

Around four a.m., a surgeon in a blue gown came out of the OR and pulled off his mask and cap. We huddled around him.

"Mr. Tipton is alive and stable. We've removed the shotgun pellets, sutured up the damage, and put him on IV antibiotics. He has a concussion from falling, but I didn't see a fracture. But the loss of blood, and the shock from the shooting has left him in a coma."

Ann started crying. I felt the poisonous losses of the past working their way through my bloodstream.

"What are the odds he'll come out of it?" Bill asked.

"Good. Sometimes a coma is the body's way of conserving energy to facilitate healing."

"Any permanent damage?" Bill asked.

"We won't know until he comes out of the coma. Go home and get some sleep. You look exhausted. I don't need any more patients."

I woke up at nine, went to the refrigerator and selected an Eskimo Cheese Whip; depression doesn't want wholesome, it wants sugar and fat. I called the hospital—no change, stable but still unconscious.

Mustering what was left of my mental agility, I got the mail—a postcard from my dentist, a polite man who always asks how I've been, reminding me that I haven't accomplished anything in half a year. The most I could point to was a series of failed attempts at advanced education, a Fluke CD still not finished, and a few trial memberships at health clubs.

I settled onto the couch in front of the TV. I'd moved back home with my brother four years ago, just after Mom died, one year after my wife left me, and thirteen years after Dad died. The home was in the middle of a tract outside Celtic City, but clearly distinguished from neighboring homes by a completely different house number.

When I was ten years old, Bill nine, and Corky twelve, our cocker spaniel puppy Kirby ran out into the street. All our cocker spaniel puppy Kirby ran out into the street. All I could do was shout "No!" and watch as Dad swerved into a utility pole. Car shrapnel hit Kirby.

A vet put Kirby to sleep so he wouldn't suffer. Dad wasn't so lucky. For two weeks the doctors tried to bring his pain under control.

"Son," he choked out one day during visiting hours, "I need rest. Okay?"

"Sure, Dad." But I couldn't leave. Couldn't say good-bye.

His eyes widened and his hand went slack. A tear formed in his eye. Whether because he'd asked me to leave and I hadn't, or because of his physical condition, I never was certain. He slipped into unconsciousness.

Back home, in bed, staring at the opposite wall, I cried, though not for long. Exhaustion dropped me into oblivion. The phone call pulled me out.

Dad had died.

At that moment, time stopped. Jimmy Carter was President, *The Official Preppie Handbook* was the rage, the question "Who shot J.R.?" had the nation guessing, Mount St. Helens and the Moral Majority were spouting off, and bumper stickers said things like *Historians Are a Thing of the Past*.

That night I listened to Mama crying to herself in her room, and I cried along with her in mine.

Over the next few years I mostly stayed inside and watched television. Sometimes Mom sat with me, but I could tell she wasn't really interested in the shows. She'd always try to strike up a conversation, first talking about nothing in particular, then asking why I didn't go out and play, and could she do anything to help me in any way.

She couldn't. I'd developed a belief in emotional distance, distance maintained by joking my way through each day, as if life were a sitcom.

Now, Eskimo Cheese Whip in hand, I watched a talk-show host and his audience debating sex-change operations with an intensity that suggested almost everyone might have one.

A commercial came on: a woman washing her hair, hinting your own hair would fall out by the handful if you didn't use Laurel shampoo. It reminded me that Laurel used the Draize Eye Irritancy Test, a national standard since 1944. Cosmetic companies place thousands of rabbits in stocks to prevent them from clawing at their eyes to dislodge toxic substances. Rabbits have no tear ducts and cannot make tears. With only their heads protruding, the lower lid of each rabbit's eye is pulled away from the eyeball to form a small cup. Into that cup a lab worker drops drain cleaner and other harsh chemicals to be tested as the rabbit squirms to break free. The eye is held closed. The rabbits, who vocalize only when in unbearable pain, scream.

I started flipping channels.

I stopped when I saw a reporter standing in front of the charred remains of the Terrig Test Lab interviewing Beezil Terrig and his wife Margo. Beezil had tiny black eyes and the slick sloping forehead of a killer whale. His wife was sobbing into a handkerchief.

"—to my knowledge," Beezil was saying, "our testing was in compliance with all regulations regarding lab animals."

"Your daughter was an animal-rights activist. Why did she burn down *your* laboratory?"

"Kristin didn't fall for that animal-rights propaganda. We raised her to be smarter than that."

"But our sources say—"

"Your sources are wrong. Besides, animals aren't even the issue, jobs are. Why don't you ever report the good side of what we do? We perform research for the benefit of all mankind."

Shaving lotion scented like urinal cakes is a giant leap for mankind?

"Your daughter must have believed otherwise."

"Listen! Kristin wasn't a fanatic about animals."

"Then perhaps she was trying to get even with you."

"What the hell for? Listen, you've got a lot of nerve."

"Something you did to her. A family problem?"

Beezil seemed taken aback by a question insinuating a dark side to his personal life. He cleared his throat. "No family problem. If Kristin *ever* supported animal-rights, she was led astray."

"By whom, Mr. Terrig?"

"I don't know. But I *will* find out." His nostrils flared into the camera and I felt as though he were looking directly at me.

"Do you feel responsible for her death?"

Beezil's head dropped. His wife stepped forward.

"We haven't been close to her for several years."

I leaned back. Kristin's parents had no idea how she felt. Maybe she'd never had a chance to tell them, or maybe they hadn't listened, but I knew she'd want them to understand her passion.

Hoover snorted, shook himself, padded over to me, and lay down. I brushed him as I waited for the Terrigs to return home. After an hour, I called, not sure if I was calling for Kristin or spoiling for a fight.

"Mrs. Terrig, I was a friend of Kristin's, and I'm very sorry about what happened."

"Thank you. It's a difficult time for us."

"I saw you on television, and if you'll allow me, I'd like to share with you the details of what Kristin believed in. It was an important part of who she was."

"Please excuse me for a moment."

I heard Beezil's angry voice in the background. I caught "animal-rights puke" and "hunting trip" before she picked the phone back up.

"We want to meet with you. There's a lot that doesn't make sense to us, but my husband will be busy for several days. We'd like to invite you to our home."

"Could we set a firm time?"

"Thursday, say at seven?"

"Thank you."

***

At dusk, for the first time in hours, my face didn't hurt so much. That was something to be glad about as Bill worked the Ford van through light traffic in Tory Town while baring his firespewing soul about Richard getting shot. When he ran out of words, he slammed his fist against the steering wheel. The glove compartment burst open and a stack of road maps slid against Hoover's legs. This derailed his anger. I arranged the maps in a neat pile and put them back.

Hoover's nose was pushed into the inch of open window I'd cracked for him. He relied on me to describe the sights.

"To our right, all along Constitution Avenue, Christmas lights are blinking off and on. Benches, awnings, telephone booths—everything is decorated with fringes of icicles reflecting the lights."

I didn't tell him that the colorful lights couldn't hide the shabbiness of the storefronts, or that the streets were infested with pushers, hookers, and reporters, each making a living off the others, or that you could walk ten blocks in any direction without leaving the scene of a crime.

As Bill turned a corner I said, "Does Ann have a boy-friend now?"

"I don't know. She rarely talks with anyone, even Corky, about anything personal."

"No one comes to gigs with her."

"Maybe she's just too busy to have a personal life. I hear it's overrated anyway."

"She spends a lot of time on child-abuse cases."

"There might be a personal reason for that."

"You think?"

"Sure. Wouldn't it be logical—if she was an abused child or something."

My stomach lurched as if Bill had shifted from fourth to reverse accidentally.

"She's never said anything like that."

"Yeah, well, it's not something likely to be real easy to talk about. You know, some psychologists say people who are crazy about animals often are that way because their fellow humans have hurt them badly."

I believed that.

"Why are you asking, anyway?"

"Just wondering."

"You never 'just wondered' anything in your life."

"I think she likes me."

"No offense, Clark, but hasn't she noticed the *TV Guide* in your back pocket?"

The hidden truth in the remark stung.

"What brought this on?"

"I picked up some blips on my radar screen."

"Such as?"

"She's trying to stop me from eating too much. Seems to want to understand my idiosyncrasies."

"I guess anything is possible," he said, then muttered to himself about there being no accounting for taste.

He parked the van, we locked up, then crossed an icy parking lot to Chez Beagle. Although it looked like a place where you'd rent a donkey, Bill had been eating here over a decade and had introduced me to the place after I got Hoover. The food came out of a microwave, but the owner was French and, as in many restaurants in France, dogs were welcome.

When we walked in, dogs shifted restlessly, their tags jingling like sleigh bells. Hoover followed us to our table, which sat, give or take a little, just inside the men's room. I picked up a copy of the local tabloid newspaper, the *Beacon Hill Examiner* from a nearby table. It would be better, on the whole, than thinking.

Across from us, nursing a bowl of soup, an old man sat in a wrinkled gray suit. On the floor beside him stretched a scruffy bundle of bones lightly sprinkled with brown fur. A tuft of beige fuzz stood up on his head and gave Bones the look of something drawn by Dr. Seuss. Bones slowly chewed on a hard dinner roll while eyeing Hoover.

After the waitress took our orders, I unfolded the *Examiner*. The headline exploded in front of me: DAUGHTER DIES IN TERRIG FIRE.

My misgivings grew when I noticed Slim Twitchle's byline over the story. While psychologists say you are your own worst critic, in Fluke's case it's always been Slim Twitchle. He reviewed us often, and seemed to take genuine pleasure in tearing us apart. When he referred to our "songs," the quotation marks around "songs" functioned much like the jaws of a Pooper Scooper.

According to Cavalry's Fire Chief, someone had cut open a gas line to a hydrogen furnace, splashed gasoline around the lab and set it on fire. Kristin died when the hydrogen exploded.

At least it must have been quick.

Beezil Terrig disputed the fire chief's explanation, claiming the gas line had burst and ignited on its own, and that he intended to sue the manufacturer.

Well, well. Is Beezil protecting Kristin? Hiding the fact his lab was the target of animal-rights activists? Or trying to make a buck off the manufacturer?

The medical examiner was calling the death accidental. Slim pointed out that a "friend of the victim" had told him that Kristin had been acting on orders from the Animal Liberation Front, connected with the local rock band Fluke. But Beezil Terrig denied that his daughter was ever part of any "animal-rights cult."

"Know anything about Kristin's personal life? Her friends?"

"No," Bill said, unsnaggling the tines of his fork. "Why?"

"Someone told Slim Twitchle that Kristin was killed while working with the A.L.F. and Fluke."

Bill looked as if someone had just crapped inside his Pope John Paul lunch box. "An inside leak would destroy us." Bill stopped talking as a waitress passed. "We have to plug it. Maybe start with Slim."

I tossed the newspaper onto the seat next to me. "I do believe I'd like to jump down Slim's throat, grab his toes, pull him inside out, and make him swallow himself." Of course, as I had no idea what he looked like, it was only an assumption that this hadn't already been done. "He probably won't help us. We need to tackle it from the direction of Kristin's friends."

"But our only connection to her is through her parents. How do we get their help?"

I couldn't, but I knew Bill could. I told him about Mr. Terrig's upcoming hunting trip.

Bill looked at the tines of his fork, now parallel. He brightened. "That gives me a long shot to learn what's been leaked."

"Can you get on the hunt?"

"I can get names off the hunting license register at the local gun shop. I'll say I'm new in town and ask if I can join them."

"I knew you'd have a plan." He was an accomplished member of the Hunt Saboteurs Association. With his hair under a cap, he did a convincing Redneck impersonation, spouting knowledge of Big Time Wrestling and the attributes of the county's best trucking institutes. He even had a Christmas card in his wallet from Red-Man chewing tobacco. "What will you do?"

"I'd bet Kristin has had her friends sabotage previous hunting trips. Those friends may be the leak. So, on the hunt, I'll ask about previous hunts. Make a few wisecracks about those commie animal-rights activists. Whatever might get Terrig shooting his mouth off if he knows anything."

"You're not afraid he'll recognize you?"

"What, you think he's a fan of ours?"

"No. But Kristin might have had some pictures of Fluke. Beezil could've found them."

"I'm more worried an ex-A.L.F. member will be on the hunt and spot what I'm doing."

The waitress slid two peanut butter sandwiches in front of us, along with Beagle's special preserves (made fresh each day by pouring jam from a can into a fancy jar) and two cups of coffee.

I was sipping mine, which tasted like something you'd sit in to remove a tattoo, when the door burst open and smashed into a plastic four-foot-high Santa holding a Styrofoam candy cane, bouncing him off the wall. To the barking of a dozen dogs, Lester Gillis, Mungo, and The Rat trampled over Santa as if storming a fortress.

"Don't show any fear," I told Bill. "Try to appear larger than you really are."

Under the table, Hoover growled low in his throat and tensed. I slipped my hand underneath his collar.

The three felons circled us. Mungo moved behind me. Looking up at him I experienced a dizzying sensation as if passing the Statue of Liberty in a rowboat. With one hand on either side of me, he leaned on the table. It sagged. Inside my stomach, half of a peanut butter sandwich did a slow somersault.

The Rat wore a buckskin cowboy jacket and boots with spurs. Before sitting down he took an apple from a bowl on the counter and started peeling it with a knife considerably larger than necessary for the job. Lester sat at the end of our table, snatched the rest of my sandwich, and swallowed it with a sound like a plumber unstopping a toilet.

"First you play your crap at the Lobster, then you steal my customers, and now you brainwash them into screwing with research you're too dumb to understand." His eyes dared me to contradict him.

I did. Perhaps because I was hungry and he'd eaten my sandwich. I raised my voice. "Those animals suffer every day! You want us to sit back and do nothing when there are cruelty free ways of testing products? Many companies use computer simulations just fine. Don't you tell me I'm too dumb to understand."

He burped. "Who gives a shit."

"What a common philosophy: don't worry about things that can't hurt you. Animals get tortured. Not your concern. But you know what *can* hurt you? Your attitude can bite you in the ass. When kids are raised with no compassion, why shouldn't they gun you down as they drive by? Believe me there is a correlation, so wise up. Try reading. It's amazing how sophisticated pop-up books have become."

I looked hard at him, impressed with my courage but appalled by my judgment. It would have been smarter to have offered him a hammer, nails, and a cross, then put my feet together.

Bones stopped chewing his dinner roll and cocked his head as if thinking over what I'd said. Lester didn't bother to.

"Just because I don't shovel it as fast as you do, doesn't mean you're right."

Mungo dope-slapped the back of my head. "Message for you, Baby Cakes. Keep your mouth shut about whatever you imagined you saw in Terrig's lab, and keep your jerkwads away from there unless you want the world to know who's in the A.L.F."

Lester was smiling. "People like *Ann Berlin* and *Corky Baker*."

I would have staggered, but I was sitting.

I turned to Bill, whose demeanor was rather like that of one who, picking daisies on the railway, had just caught the Amtrak in the small of the back.

"A.L.F. members don't use their *real* names," I said.

Mungo rubbed the back of his hand across his mouth. "Bullshit, Baby Cakes."

That's a nickname I sure hope doesn't stick.

Lester made a slight upward gesture with his hand and all three felons rose.

As they headed for the door, Bones growled softly. Without breaking stride, Lester kicked him in the head with a sickening thud that sent the dog yelping under his master's chair.

I've learned to live with many of my mistakes—a campaign contribution to Bob Packwood, buying my wife a Dirt Devil for Valentines—but I felt guilty about making Lester mad enough to kick that poor old dog. Bones had abandoned his dinner roll and now seemed afraid of it.

If Lester comes back, I'll stuff that roll so far up his butt that the Donner Party wouldn't reach it on a three day hike.

When my legs were steady, I pushed myself into a standing position, put money on the table, helped Santa to his feet, and went outside into the chilly night, where the clash of Renaissance armies was only sleet beating on the aluminum awnings.

"You know," Bill said, "you haven't heard the last of what happened back there."

"You sound pretty certain."

"I am. If you ever get married again, when the judge asks, 'Is there any reason these two shouldn't be married,' I'm going to say 'Does she know he's *insane?*' and tell them about this."

The issue of my sanity sounded like dangerous territory, so I declared a personal moratorium on the subject and instead asked, "How did Lester know we were here?"

"You think he's been tailing us?"

"Unless someone at Beagle tipped him off."

"Doubt that. Those people have been my good friends for a very long time."

Lester may have unspeakable ways of persuading them, I thought.

But my worried expression must have confused Bill, because he sounded defensive. "Clark, you're my best friend. You know that, don't you?"

I looked from side to side like a dog who needed to be let out.

"I love you," he said.

Go on. Tell him you love him, too. I started to. I nearly did.

Bill was in the kitchen taking shrink-wrap off three new Bibles, Dudley was looking out the window, and Ann was talking about Richard winning the Cavalry city cleanup prize in 1993 and 1996. In her voice was a rising wistfulness at the sense of something good having come to an end. Tears formed in her eyes and ran down her cheeks.

Corky hugged her. "Me, too. I've been locking myself in bathrooms and crying."

"Sounds like a good name for a country music song," I said, but wished I hadn't. This was no time to joke. Dudley was looking out of the window at passing cars. Maybe thinking of throwing himself into the road.

Bill handed me a bible—he gave them to people who needed "a good talking-to from the Lord." I had an impressive collection.

After a long silence I spoke softly, telling them about my conversation with Mrs. Terrig.

"We owe it to Kristin to tell them. And I know you caring folks will insist on joining me when I go over there."

"Sorry," Bill said. "You're chafing your lips on the wrong butt."

I glanced around the room at the others.

Dudley brushed his hand through his thick black hair.

"And what, exactly, aren't you telling us?"

"Nothing much, really. A friend of Kristin's seems to have leaked the names of several A.L.F. members, and Beezil hired Lester Gillis to threaten us to keep quiet."

Anger flowed out of Dudley like a tangible force.

"Hell. I'll go with you then. In fact, I'll run over there right now and punch him in the mouth." Dudley punched at a folding metal chair. He barely touched it, but it buckled comically and crashed with a clatter.

"When you're finished with the chair," I said, "I have a mixing board that's been giving me trouble."

"Why resort to violence, Dudley?" Ann was serious. "You're smarter than Beezil is."

"Oh, good. Then I'll dash right over and give him a pop quiz."

"Kristin deserves having her parents understand what she believed in," Ann said. "I'll go with you, Clark."

"That's nice," Bill said, "and I'm sure her dad will sincerely thank you both to a pulp."

"We still have to find the leak," Dudley said.

Corky headed for the door. "How about if I call each A.L.F. member and ask if they'll lead the Laurel mission. If anyone balks without a fast reason, we'll know to be suspicious."

"What if they agree only so they can lead us into a trap?"

"Good point. We'll change plans at the last minute to mess them up. Let's visit Richard."

Outside, Hoover arfed and snapped at the snow like he knew he should be playing in it, but wasn't quite sure what to do. I wished I could teach him to frolic. When I said "Okay," he jumped into the van. I tucked him under a blanket, and with only his nose sticking out, he seemed at peace with the world.

As Highway 1 threaded its way northeast between rolling hills, gusts of wind tried to push us into snow banks in the gully below. Corky sat next to me in the front and slid the Miles Davis CD we'd bought for Richard into the player. It choked me up a little, listening to what Richard liked.

Dudley leaned forward and touched Corky's shoulder. "What'll it take to get you to go on a date?"

"You got any friends?"

Dudley started to laugh, but his breath caught short when he noticed a pair of ducks flying north, fighting the wind driven snow. "Loons are very rare in Massachusetts. Especially flying after sunset."

Corky squinted in the direction of the birds.

"Six pairs nest at the Quabbin reservoir," Dudley went on, "and four near the reservoir. Acid rain is threatening their habitat . . ." About five minutes into Dudley's monologue on the trials and tribulations of loons, Ann and Bill had dozed off, tilting against each other.

The windshield wipers weren't coping well with the snow flying straight into the windshield like tracer bullets. I switched on the high beams, turning the snow into a white curtain. I switched back to low.

Something in my rearview mirror broke through the haze. A car was gaining on us, fast. My speed had crept up to fifty. I slowed to forty, moved into the right lane and held steady.

Instead of passing, the driver slowed down and paced us, staying in my blind spot.

What's his problem? I increased my speed to fifty, back to forty. He did the same. Now I was worried.

With patches of ice on the road, I was afraid to make a sudden move. The car, a white Celica, increased speed and drew even with me. Through murky darkness and two fogged windows I saw a tight-lipped grimace.

He began moving ahead of me. *Have I driven him to road*

rage?

With that thought lodged in my head like a bullet, he started moving into my lane, forcing me off the road.

I backed off the accelerator. He matched my speed and continued edging into me, so I gambled and pumped the brakes.

The Celica swerved into us and its right rear bumper clipped the van. An agonizing cry of shredding metal was followed by a shattering of glass as the van's left headlight was pulverized.

We shot toward the frozen ravine that ran parallel to the highway, nearly fifty feet below.

I pulled hard to the left.

The van began to tilt, and I corrected with a slight pull to the right and a tap on the brakes. The energy of the aborted rollover channeled itself into a slide. When I tried to correct, the van slithered like a wet bar of soap from one side of the highway to the other until we plunged over the shoulder.

I was still fighting the wheel as we slued down an embankment. The front passenger door flew open. I clung to the steering wheel. Corky grappled with the dashboard and struggled to stay inside as objects hurled past her, out the door.

So this is it, curtains. And the show was just getting interesting. On to the Afterlife. *I'm sure I'll go to heaven, I've been dull enough.*

My head hit the steering wheel.

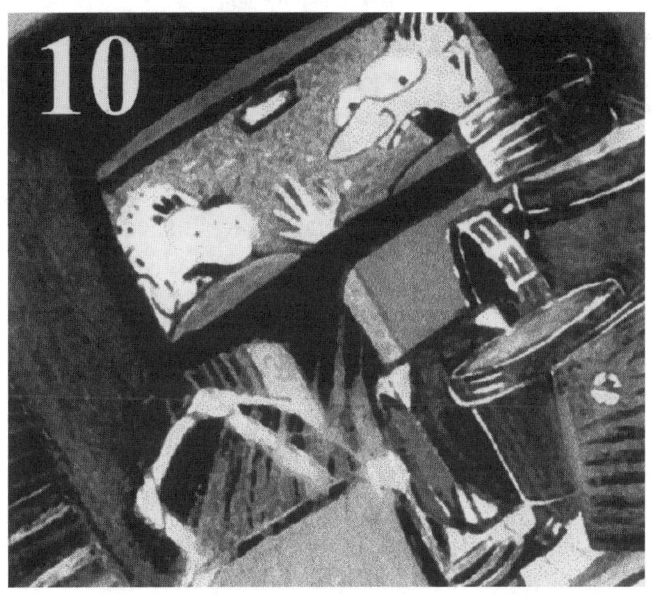

Heaven was a snow bank and an ice-encrusted maple tree. Looking out the windshield I gazed up at a shimmering guitar, dangling like ripe fruit from a low branch.

An angelic creature tugged at my arm.

Corky. I shook my head to clear it, but I might as well have been trying to finish a jigsaw puzzle by shaking the box. Gripping my arm, Corky pulled herself upright, taking me back down to earth at the same time. Although still dizzy, I now understood that the guitar-bearing-tree was only some sort of prank, or perhaps an advertisement that (like most others) I did not understand.

"You okay?" I asked, as a headache began to crack down the center of my forehead.

"Next time, I drive," my sister said. "Not that I don't just love the inside of your glove compartment."

I twisted around. Ann was rubbing her eyes.

"What happened?"

"Someone tried to kill us," Dudley said. "If Clark hadn't kept us on the road till we passed that ravine—"

"You all right?" I asked Ann.

"What about you?" She touched my forehead. "It's bleeding."

"Who the hell was that?" Bill was looking out the windows. "Is he still around?"

Corky climbed out into the blackness. I followed. Steam hissed from under the van, and a car sloshed by up on the road; no flashlight searched for us, no Celica lurked. Snow was blowing in on the rising wind, closing our footprints like dents in dough.

A smothered whimper cleared my dizziness instantly.

"Hoover!"

I stumbled to the rear of the van. The doors hung open. Papers, boxes, and a spare tire littered the snow. I groped from one dark shape to another until I spotted him, facedown and motionless under a broken amplifier. I tossed it aside with a strength I'd never before had, unprepared to deal with the loss of another friend.

His blood stained the snow. I thought I saw his rib cage move, but it could've just been the wind. I put my hand on his neck and could feel, weak and irregular, a heartbeat.

His body convulsed.

"Please Hoover, hold on."

I fumbled in my pockets for the keys, then realized they would still be in the ignition. I forced myself to breathe, got seated and cranked the engine.

Everyone strained, rocking the van, trying to loosen it from the trench it had carved in the snow.

Bill shouted, "Hoover lifted his head."

My shaking slowed. I cranked again. The engine turned over but didn't start.

Corky stuck her head through an open window. "You and I can hitchhike to the last town we passed. The others can dig the van out. If they free the van before we get a ride, they can pick us up." She was taking charge. It felt right.

When I approached Hoover, he tried to wag his tail.

I took off my jacket, wrapped it around him, positioned my

hand under his furry body and lifted him into the crook of my arm. Although he didn't resist me, he made a pained sound.

"Easy." Cradling him tightly, I said, "Corky and I are hitch-hiking to a vet."

Dudley looked at the buried van.

"Look for us in half-an-hour."

Ann touched Corky's shoulder. "I know where Dr. Dean lives. I'll go."

"Good," Corky said. "I'll help here. Watch for that car to return."

I'd seen a white Toyota driving around near Terrig Corporation the night Kristin died. Maybe he hadn't been lost. *Maybe Kristin's death wasn't an accident.*

Dudley came up behind me and wrapped his nylon jacket over my shoulders.

"Thanks."

Ann and I worked our way up the embankment. A ribbon of blood matted the fur by Hoover's nose. I tried not to jostle him. He turned a panting mouth and a confused expression up to me as if expecting me to stop the pain. I wished I could explain to him that not even a big dog like me could do that.

We reached the shoulder of the highway and started walking. My wet clothes began to stiffen. Minutes passed. I hugged Hoover, who was getting colder and heavier.

The sound of an engine cut through the swooshing wind. Ann turned and stuck out her thumb. I stroked Hoover's side but couldn't feel any warmth or movement. *Is he alive?* It was a prayer.

A Cadillac Narcissus whuffed by without even slowing down. It nearly hit us. Its driver scowled like we'd been stationed on the side of the highway just to annoy him. Angered, I shouted in his wake, "May your hemorrhoids win prizes at county fairs!"

The next car was moving slower, more deliberately. Ann put her thumb out again and the car slid to a stop just past us. Rusty and dented, it reminded me of the Dumpster behind

Chez Beagle. Clutching Hoover's dead weight to my chest, I ran after Ann, who opened the rear door, jumped in, and held the door open for me.

I handed Hoover to her, got in, then took him back. He stirred. *He's alive.* A warm glow flowed through me.

The driver twisted and leaned over the seat. She was wearing what looked like a nightgown, but was apparently an evening gown. Sheer, black, with layers of ruffles down the front.

"Hi. I'm Joy."

Ann introduced us, and I thanked Joy as much as I could, short of saying I loved her, which might have been misconstrued.

"You the accident back there?"

"'Fraid so."

She touched Hoover's shoulder.

"Is he okay?"

"We need to get him to a vet."

"Hang on." Joy eased back onto the icy highway, punched the accelerator and we took off. The headlights made an empty tunnel into the darkness ahead of us. By the light of the occasional street lamp I saw blood trickling from Hoover's muzzle. I held him tightly.

The dashboard clock said 8:45 when we hit downtown Plymouth, which was brightly lit but mostly empty, like a movie set. Ann told Joy the address. We were passing through a residential area when Joy suddenly turned into a driveway. "Here we are." She pointed to a modest wooden sign, ROBERT B. DEAN AND SON, VETERINARIANS. "Take care."

"We will," Ann said. "Bye-bye. And thanks."

As I slid out with Hoover, I smeared blood on the upholstery. "Sorry."

"Get in there," she said, looking like one of those big-eyed, dark-haired children with the sad expressions you see painted on velvet. She gave me a little wave as she drove off. I waved back. Somehow it seemed sad that she would never know how anything turned out.

Ann rang the front doorbell. The porch light came on, the door opened, and Dr. Dean stood before us in a faded tan bathrobe. Without saying a word he gently took Hoover and marched down a hallway. Ann and I followed him through a door at the end of the hall.

He lay Hoover on an examining table. Ann held her hand out to me, and when I let my hand slip into hers, she pulled me gently away. Dr. Dean listened to Hoover's heart and lungs with a stethoscope, palpated his abdomen, and examined his wounds. Hoover lay stiffly on his side, as if paralyzed. The only signs he clung to life were his ragged breathing and faint whimpers.

Dr. Dean went to a cabinet and took out a needle. I knew what that meant. I must have gasped because he glanced up. "It's only a painkiller. For now. The next several hours will be critical."

Hoover remained stiff, tongue lolling, muscles tense. With agonizing slowness, Dr. Dean inserted the needle. Hoover didn't move, but as the plunger went down his muscles began to relax.

I wouldn't let another loved one die without saying good-bye. I put my lips close to his ear.

"Good-bye, Hoover."

He lifted his head suspiciously. *Was I finally going to betray him?* his expression asked.

"You're a good dog." I had trouble keeping my voice steady. "I love you very, very much."

Hoover whined softly. He knew that. He knew some things very clearly. He knew Love. He knew Friend. But he didn't understand Good-bye. No pack animal does, not even for a minute.

"See you when you wake up."

Dr. Dean set down the needle and directed us into his kitchen. Ann sat on the edge of a chair, and I performed a caged-lion imitation.

"When I was fifteen," she said, "my collie, Topper, got out of the back yard."

I stopped pacing.

"I combed the streets for days," she said. "Then a clerk at an animal shelter told me they'd gotten a collie but kept him only six hours. She described the collie and I was sure he was my Topper. But she wouldn't break regulations and tell me who took him—until I started crying. He'd been turned over to a laboratory for animal experimentation—only ten blocks away."

Her eyes flickered as she seemed to look inward. "I ran all ten blocks to the lab. While I was screaming *bloody murder* at the receptionist, Topper began barking from behind a locked door. I pried the door open, but two security guards dragged me out.

"I cried for weeks, certain it had been a terrible mistake. Years later I found out that pound-seizure laws force animal shelters to turn over lost cats and dogs to experimentation—more than 200,000 a year. So I joined the A.L.F. and went to law school to learn how to fight the bastards who make laws like that."

Her hair sagged on her head, her head sagged on her shoulders. "Time has gone by so fast." She sat in a sort of limp, crumpled way, as if she'd been hurled onto her chair from a passing train. "So little has changed."

Time had gotten away from both of us. I thought about what Dad had missed by dying in 1980. *What would he have thought of personal computers, Rubik's Cube, Baby Fae, MTV, and Lake Wobegon?*

Pacing in front of the kitchen window, I stared out at the darkness. All those changes and nothing prepares you for how much it hurts when someone you love dies.

11

At 9:32 there was a sharp rap on Dr. Dean's front door.

"I'll get it," I said. Then I remembered there was a man outside who'd recently attempted to turn me into road-kill. "Who is it?"

"We're soliciting donations for the morally handicapped. We accept whips, chains, live chickens, or Mike Tyson Fan Club Cards!"

"I've been waiting for you since puberty." I swung the door open.

Dudley breezed in, followed by Bill and Corky.

"Saw you pacing in front of the window," Dudley said. "Didn't you think we'd show?"

"Too wired to sit."

"How's Hoover?" Bill asked.

"Alive. Doc's with him now."

We gathered around the kitchen table. "How'd you get here so fast?"

Bill told us of how Heather had gone back for them.

Then Ann told of our bone-chilling hitchhike. I interjected

one point with which she disagreed. "That Joy's a sweet girl," I said. "Maybe a bit naïve. A young girl driving alone at night should know better than to pick up hitchhikers."

"I hate to be the one to take a flyswatter to your Tinker Bell," Ann said, "but that sweet girl is a prostitute who's had plenty of practice doing a quick read of strangers."

This dazed me. "You really think so?"

From the next room, Hoover let out a whine of pain that made me shudder. Too much good in the world seemed to be dying. Somewhere a clock ticked steadily.

Nearly an hour later, Dr. Dean carried out Hoover, limp and lifeless. My heart sank.

"Is he all right?" Ann asked.

At the sound of Ann's voice, Hoover's limp tail jerked in a fair attempt at wagging. His face, though thinner and tired, lit up.

Dr. Dean placed Hoover in Ann's outstretched arms. "Well, he's banged up pretty bad, a few cuts, probably cracked a rib or two, but there are no signs of organ damage."

I laughed with relief.

"It took fifty-eight stitches to stop the hemorrhaging." Dr. Dean took off a pair of thin rubber gloves and dropped them in a trashcan. "Blood loss was minimal. The cold weather probably saved his life. He'll need plenty of rest and clean bandages every day." He scratched Hoover's chin. Hoover licked his hand.

I followed him to the surgery room where he handed me gauze, a bottle of hydrogen peroxide and another of antibiotics, and the bill.

Riding home in a taxi, I watched the landscape driven with snow as the wind whistled across untouched drifts. The stars were flickering through thinning clouds. I did my best to describe the view to Hoover.

* * *

That night I lay awake in bed and listened to Hoover's soft breathing. When I closed my eyes I could see Beezil's killer-whale face. He would battle us with all the resources of the Terrig Corporation. A battle we couldn't avoid, yet a battle we couldn't win with a leak in the A.L.F. I stared at the ceiling, a Howard Jones' song running through my head.

As long as there are slaughterhouses, there will be battle-fields

As long as animals die in testing, we won't find humanity
Don't be part of it, don't be part of the killing.

The only part of me that slept at all that night was my right hand. And that was only because it was wrapped around a baseball bat so tightly that God Himself would've broken a few fingernails trying to get it away from me.

***

Hoover nestled between Ann and the passenger window. His head drooped over the edge of the front seat, bangs falling over his eyes. The van had been dragged back up to the road, where, minus some chrome and glass, it ran just fine.

When we arrived at Paul Revere Hospital, Dudley volunteered to stay in the van with Hoover.

The afternoon sun shone on the pool around the statue of Paul Revere that graced the entrance to the hospital. The water in the pool was black, and a sign hanging around the neck of Paul Revere's horse read, "Danger. Pond contains antifreeze." Sparrows who couldn't read were preening their feathers and drinking, heads tilted back into the sun with each beakful of poison.

Inside the hospital, thirty yards past the nurses' station, Bill, Ann, and I walked into a white, sterile room. Richard stared without recognition out of unblinking eyes. An IV dripped clear liquid into the vein in his arm. Ann's gaze fixed on the large purplish bruise on his forehead. She dabbed at a tear. I didn't cry, but my eyes itched.

We listened to Richard breathe in, breathe out.

I pulled a white plastic chair close beside him and took his right hand. He didn't stir. His fingers stayed limp, but at least they were warm.

As I held his hand, my mind drifted back four years: The Lobster had been a typical nightclub, and Fluke a typical self-absorbed rock band, neither connected with the A.L.F. Although I'd gone along with Corky on A.L.F. missions, I had never discussed them with anyone else, even my brother. One night after the Lobster had closed, Richard came up to us as we were packing our equipment.

"I'll donate fifty percent of the gate to the A.L.F., if you'll play two extra nights a week."

Only Bill voted no, saying it would make it too hard to play weekends in New York, but he accepted the outcome.

Later, I caught Richard in his office.

"What made you decide to support the A.L.F.?"

"I've always wondered what rationale people like Klansmen applied to draw a line around one group of beings and claim they had more innate worth than others. I was talking with your sister yesterday and suddenly saw that I, too, drew a line around a group of beings— human beings."

"But you know that not every A.L.F. action is legal. Breaking the law isn't your style."

"The A.L.F.'s actions are no different from those of abolitionists before the Civil War, when slavery laws and even the Supreme Court said owning humans was legal. In the end, who turned out to be morally right?"

That was as philosophical a statement as I'd ever heard Richard utter.

Now I was afraid I'd never hear another. Richard breathed in, and out.

"Who shot you?" I whispered. "Give me a sign. Was it the purple-haired guy who jumped onstage?" Richard's face didn't change. "Lester Gillis? Some guy in a white Toyota? Some buddy of Granite's?"

Ann said, "Granite was chatting with Mervyn like they were old friends. Maybe Mervyn knows what Granite was up to."

A nurse whisked into the room, checked the monitor, transcribed the information onto Richard's chart, then left.

"Can you hear me, Richard?" His breathing was barely audible. I studied his face for any movement, any sign. "Please wake up. Please tell me who shot you." *Please don't die.*

I couldn't fight the déjà vu. It was more than just that this was the same hospital where my father had died. Until now I hadn't understood how much I'd come to depend upon their positive outlooks. Their moods always brought mine up.

Although, right now, so would the moods of Kafka and Edgar Allen Poe.

Did Richard blink? I leaned closer to him, but saw only the movement of his lungs letting each breath out, pausing, then drawing another one in.

We breathed together. In, and out. In, and out. In, then *sharply* out! That's when I knew he was going to make it. When his breathing changed ever so slightly, ever so consciously.

"Richard?"

His eyes fluttered . . . then actually opened for a moment.

Bill and Ann crowded around the bed. Richard squinted, then focused on me. I touched his forehead.

"Hey, buddy."

"Anyone else get hurt?" His voice was barely audible; his lips barely moved.

"No."

"Thank God."

"How do you feel?"

"Numb." He made a small movement as if to sit up, and winced. "Ow. Not numb enough."

"Don't move," Ann said. "Just rest."

"Do you remember getting shot?" Bill asked.

Richard frowned. "Vaguely. I went to my office. The door was open, but it was dark. I stepped inside . . . the blast felt close. A fireball, high. . . ."

"Did you see who did it?"

Richard closed his eyes and slowly shook his head.

"Has anyone threatened you?" Bill asked.

Richard's eyes opened with concern, and then I realized, with his positive nature, he'd never considered that possibility.

"I assumed it was a thief and I was blocking his escape." He paused. "Will you take care of the Lobster for me?"

I stiffened.

"Please?" he asked.

Does he think he is going to die?

Richard yawned. "Just until I get out of here."

"Gladly. What do you want us to do?"

"Put up a 'closed for renovation' sign. Maybe shovel some snow so it doesn't look deserted."

The nurse reappeared and called for a doctor, who welcomed Richard back and ordered an EEG. The nurse wheeled in a monitoring device and taped small pinkish electrodes to Richard's forehead. Her practiced face revealed no hint of what the waveforms were telling her. I kept asking what the various gauges indicated. She answered my first few questions and then made a gesture like urging a baby bird to fly.

I moved to the door and cleared my throat. "I'm going to find the gunman."

Bill's jaws gaped slowly, as if held by a weak spring.

Ann asked, "You're going to look for him *now?*"

"I don't think you should be looking for him, period," Bill said. "He's probably left Massachusetts. Not that it matters. You couldn't arrest him if he jumped out of your breakfast cereal. Let the police do it. Find softer walls to beat your head against."

"The police'll be too busy following *us* to find him. And I know motives that don't translate well."

"Still, detectives need special powers of observation."

"What am I? Deaf and dumb?"

"Nothing personal, Clark. It's just that you trust people too much. You're not suspicious enough. You take people at face value. You don't look under the surface."

What do you say about me when I'm not IN the room?

I started to climb up on my high horse, but caught myself in time. As a divorced man whose very first clue that his marriage wasn't perfect came a year after his wife had started dating a lawyer, I was in no position to convince Bill how sharp my powers of observation were.

"Isn't it worth taking a shot?"

Bill delivered a cool stare at me. "I don't mean to be condescending, Alice, but you seem to be viewing things from the wrong side of the Looking Glass. It's the shots I'm worried about. Because we may already be the *target*. Besides, there's a lot to do over the next four days. Do you think it's even remotely possible you could support the A.L.F. on this?"

"No."

"Thanks for mulling it over." He looked as if I'd slapped him.

"Why seek revenge?" Ann said softly. "If you retaliate with violence, you'll become one of *them*. I know you've lost a great deal. But if you attack them you'll have lost something irreplaceable."

"Yeah," Bill said. "You'll have lost your mind."

"It's not revenge I'm after," I said. "It's answers. It's critical we know the gunman's motive. If he wanted to stop Fluke, maybe he's reached his goal. But if he wants to stop the A.L.F., he may have just begun. That's why finding him is more important than any *single* A.L.F. mission. So I'll see you later."

Snow had padded the parking lot with several inches of silence, but the sky was clearing. Dudley opened the van door before I reached it. He probably knew by the look on my face that something was wrong.

He didn't say anything, just nodded and rushed toward the hospital.

"Come on, Hoover."

I dragged out my metal suitcase of spare gig supplies, including clothes.

"Let's find a room near the Lobster. The gunman might return." *That's my hope. As the saying goes, hope is what makes life worth while.* Something had to make life worth while, and that's what I chose.

Hoover waddled along close behind me down Washington Avenue, past George's Cutoff, and along the perimeter of George's Cemetery (conveniently close to the hospital without actually being visible to the patients). Black-garbed mourners drifted like forlorn spirits away from an open grave; others huddled in chairs as if prepared to stay forever with lost loved ones. As I passed a grave near the fence, my shadow shot up the headstone, startled me, and disappeared.

My theatrics hadn't fooled anyone. My friends knew I'd exaggerated the odds the gunman was attacking the A.L.F. More likely he was a burglar or a drug addict or a nut.

"I don't know why I'm seeking vengeance." My face felt hot. I had just lied to my dog.

As a kid I had sworn never to lie to myself. After Dad died, I learned that the truth can make you feel like you're in hell with your back broke, and that my sanity depended on my ability to ignore the truth. I started living my daily life hiding from the fact that the whole saga of mankind hasn't the slightest significance for the quadrillion galaxies that twinkle and roar around us. I survived because my capacity for self-delusion, like most people's, far exceeded my capacity for self-knowledge.

But I had never lied to Hoover. With his expressive face and guileless heart, with his body language and his soul-revealing tail, he was incapable of deceit.

"Okay," I said, "so I *do* know the reason."

Hoover waited. Near the end of the cemetery, small headstones in family plots bunched together like frightened cattle.

"Shooting a good man like Richard shouldn't go unpunished."

Hoover chuffed, licked his chops, and cocked his head.

"Okay, the truth. When my Dad died, something in me went with him. My Mom tried to get me interested in school, but nothing held my interest. Bill shepherded me to church for a year, but simply saying 'I have faith' seemed too easy. I returned to a life of fruitless introspection. It was Richard who first noticed my passion for music. Dad was a great guitarist and Richard suggested I should try playing professionally. So I did. Why not? By that time I wondered if my arms and legs would even move if someone else weren't pulling the strings."

Hoover still seemed to be waiting for an explanation.

"Until Richard motivated me, I often wondered if my life had any meaning beyond a somewhat sophisticated step in the recycling of carbon atoms. I don't want to return to those empty days. I have to find my own motivation. For the moment, vengeance is all I can come up with."

Hoover pointed his nose away from me, toward the street ahead, evidently satisfied with my explanation.

The farther we got from the hospital, the more I felt a deep ravine separated me from all my previous days. I was on my own. Nobody at the strings.

Fresh snow muffled my footsteps. I sometimes turned my head and looked behind me to see if anyone was following. We walked over the Gettysburg Bridge and a dozen streets lay before us, silent but for the whistling of the wind.

We came to an intersection but I wasn't sure of the direction to Rosy Street. I stood there looking at Hoover. An empty paper cup with golden arches on it skittered along the gutter, heading left. It seemed to be a sign. So I followed it.

After half a block, it plunged down a sewer.

Well, I didn't do that right away.

I looked for another sign. Daniel Boone I'm not. I'm not even Dudley Mack, who can be dropped in the middle of any city and within two hours find the town's freshest bread, a black market money changer, and a hotel with live gerbils and video cameras. Me, I was twenty miles from my birthplace and totally lost.

Hoover was beginning to pant and chuff so I picked him up. An elderly couple was walking our way. The man's cap said "Historical Site."

"Excuse me. Do you know of a hotel around here that will let me in with a dog?" Hoover began licking my face. "Oh, stop that," I said, touching my forehead to his. When I looked back up, the couple was already striding off, glancing back at me and whispering anxiously to each other about which way they would run if I came after them.

I walked past skeletons of bars and markets; half-crumbled masonry piles with dank air blowing out through scores of smashed-out windows as if the enterprises had been bombed out of business. The door of a small soup kitchen was flung open momentarily for a torrent of boiling water that splashed all over the street in a cloud of steam. A man displaying a single brown tooth approached me, a folded newspaper under his arm.

"Spare some change?"

"Funny, I was about to ask you the same thing. Why are you backing away? Where can I find a hotel that allows dogs?"

He pointed north along Hale Street with his newspaper, at the same time parrying with it to keep me away. I noticed the paper was a horse-racing form. I didn't think he had an eye for winners.

Down a side street I saw the Howling Lobster, dark and deserted. The police barricades had been taken down.

Three blocks farther I found the Suite Night Hotel.

Behind the counter in the hotel's lobby I saw myself in the cracked mirror. The lower half of my face was covered with a scruffy beard, the top half sprinkled with purple steering-wheel and knuckle welts. My lips were swollen the size of wax party gags. I heard loud snoring, and punched the bell on the counter three times before the snoring stopped with a snort. A dour desk clerk came around the corner, asked me to register, looked me over, and then demanded a month's cash in advance. When I'd produced the money, and he'd gotten over his amazement, he dropped a room key into my open palm.

"Room 300. Dog better not bark." His karma in a wringer, he headed back to his nap.

Carrying Hoover and my suitcase, I trudged up a rickety wooden stairway. Two floors up, to the left, I found "300" scrawled in felt pen on a door. I stepped inside, fondled the wall for a light switch, gave up and closed the door. All I could see was the dim outline of a bed. I was not worried; this was not the kind of hotel where you had to examine your pillow before lying down lest you wind up with a complimentary miniature chocolate lodged in your ear.

I put Hoover on the bed, plopped down next to him, and stared upward at dark shadows. When I closed my eyes, I saw Richard in the hospital. Worry carved in merciless lines on Bill's face. A tear in the corner of Ann's eye. *I won't forget a single detail of these last few days, so help me God, if I live to be normal.*

For the longest time I flopped around on the bed like a fish in the bottom of a boat, thinking disjointedly about life and death, and picking at tiny fuzzy things on the cotton blanket. I figured to have all the tiny fuzzies removed by morning.

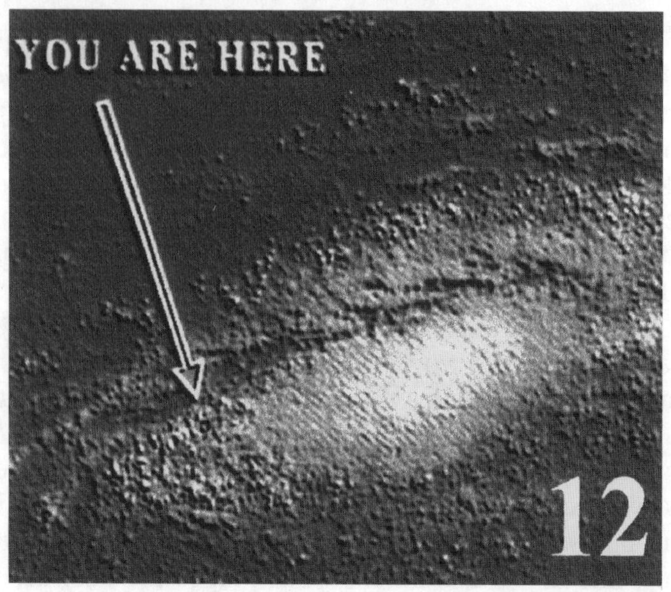

My subconscious fought wakefulness as though it were my enemy—until I felt two small paws on my arm. I stroked Hoover's head and he dug in next to me.

I stretched upward and twisted a knob on the wall. A bare bulb flickered on, revealing a painting of a dairy cow that, judging from its composition and brushwork, was a self-portrait. To my left a ratty chair, a teetering dresser, a black and white television, a steam radiator, and a junkyard coffee table sat covered by a blanket of dust. Straight ahead, an open door led to a dingy bathroom. A sheet metal counter, a small refrigerator, and a door leading to a fire escape composed the east wing.

Rolling off the bed, I thought about Kristin Terrig burning to death and Richard Tipton getting shot. I began feeling sick—physically sick. I removed my shirt, shivered in the icy air, then pulled on a fresh shirt and buttoned it wrong on the first try. When I did it wrong on the second try, I considered sitting down on the floor and giving up. In canine innocence, Hoover believed a wagging tail or an affectionate warm lick could relieve any sadness. He rubbed his flank against my legs and swished his tail. I said, "good dog," but it didn't fool him. He padded away in confusion.

In the kitchenette, dawn's first light shone through a two-foot-square window, finding no color, inside or out. Two pigeons settled on the window ledge, slowly chewing, looking at me looking at them. Adjacent to the door leading to the fire escape was a metal counter with a telephone. I called my sister, knowing she'd be getting ready for school.

"Where are you?" she asked. "Bill said you went berserk."

I must remember to thank him when there are no witnesses around. "In a hotel. What's the status of the Laurel mission?"

"On. But we need to be careful."

"What if Laurel knows we're coming?"

"They'll probably just move their test rabbits; they don't know we're after their test procedures."

"Or they'll set up an ambush."

"We'll proceed carefully. In the meantime, we've got to plug the leak." Her voice trailed off. The leak created uncertainty even her organizational skills couldn't eliminate.

I called Bill. With our futures at a crossroads, I decided that I'd tell him I loved him. Once, shortly after Dad died, my brother worked himself into such a rage over the way I distanced myself that he punched me in the chest over and over, crying all the while how much he loved me.

He still tells me. I still haven't told him, but at least he doesn't hit me anymore. I guess he's decided no amount of pounding can tenderize a tough old heart.

I got the answering machine, left a message for him to call me, and phoned Dudley.

"I'm going to stake out the Terrigs' home," he said, "see if I can catch someone from the A.L.F. coming or going, then ask him about the leaks."

"What will you say?"

"I'll ask why he's visiting Terrig, and wrong answers will lead to the inconvenience of his needing to take nutrients through a tube in the arm."

Knowledge of a crime before it happens makes one an accomplice, and since I had no desire to wake up next to a warm, affectionate body on a prison bunk, I changed the subject.

"It looks like we'll be unemployed for awhile. What are your plans?"

"I hope Corky will let me keep helping her."

"More volunteer work? Have you done the math? If you add the zero dollars the Boston Aquarium pays you to the zero dollars you'd get from the A.L.F., you won't be able to pay for your bad habits. You won't be able to even rent one for an hour."

"Gardening has always seemed a pleasant profession. All you need is a lawn mower, a weed whacker, a few simple tools. There's not much overhead, and you hardly ever get shot at."

"See you." As I hung up laughing, I pictured Ann laughing, brushing her hair behind her ears. I missed her laughter. Now, the fact I'd never called her without a business reason got thrown into sharp relief. If I called her to chat she might guess how I felt about her. And she might reveal her true feelings for me. She might tell me she likes me as a friend.

It was a tiny terror that struck me unexpectedly, like walking face-first through a spider web in the dark. I put the phone down. *I'll call her later.*

I called every automobile mechanic listed in the Yellow Pages. I gave each my phone number and asked them to watch for a white Toyota Celica with a smashed right rear bumper. There'd be a reward.

After unsticking the shower curtain from itself, I bathed in streams of brackish liquid that seemed to spurt from the rusty showerhead in every direction but mine. Then I put on my last clean pair of boxer shorts. I felt tired, lonely and, remarkably, happy.

It was a dreary morning, but warm, and the snow was

melting. I decided to slosh to the hospital while the sloshing was good. Richard might remember more about what had happened in the moments before he was shot.

Hoover followed me into the hospital lobby. Before I could ask the receptionist to keep an eye on him, she squealed with delight.

"What a cutie! Here baby."

Hoover stayed with the receptionist while I ran upstairs. The nurses told me that Richard was asleep; he'd had a rough night.

I wrote my hotel address and phone number on a piece of paper and slipped it into the pocket of his hospital gown, then squeezed his hand and said good-bye. On my way out, I thanked the receptionist for watching Hoover. She made me promise to bring him next time.

Heading home, I stopped at a newsstand. The vendor caught me staring at his ragged clothes, his eyes somehow embarrassed in their sadness. I paid him five-dollars for a copy of the *Beacon Hill Examiner*. He thanked me, but still seemed sad.

At the Jolly Lobster Bakery I bought hot chocolate and a donut, then sat in a booth near the door. Hoover lay at my feet. After reading the paper's food section, and pondering how "brash" and "adventurous" could be adjectives for cheese, I turned to the front page: CAVALRY BAR OWNER ANIMAL RIGHTS VICTIM.

That annoying Slim Twitchle again. "Richard Tipton, owner of the Howling Lobster Nightclub, was shot in yet another example of the violence that surrounds animal-rights activists. Fluke's demise may be a death blow to the local animal-rights movement, which has been spreading like wildfire." Slim concluded by quoting Cavalry's Police Chief, Patti York: "It's possible someone shot Mr. Tipton because he supported activists who were trying to close Terrig Corporation." Richard's picture accompanied the article. A younger Richard, quite a good likeness, except he was usually in better focus.

With a hot drink and a stale donut under my belt, I felt queasier but less annoyed. Hoover and I left. The sky had filled with dark clouds that seemed to return the morning to its predawn state.

"Baker."

I turned and a flashbulb blinded me. I glanced away at two hookers and a pimp hovering within knifing distance. When my eyes stopped blinking, I recognized the man behind the camera. He looked bigger standing upright than when I'd ridden him like a toboggan across an icy parking lot.

I considered once again wrestling him to the ground and questioning him rigorously. But I reconsidered this tactic when I noticed he was smiling. Over his smile, his eyes came through as a kind of radiance. Also radiating from him was the strong scent of cherry after-shave. As for me, my head still hurt. I hadn't shaved in two days and I was beginning to bear a slight family resemblance to Sirhan Sirhan.

"How are you?" Granite said.

A little crazier every day. "*Who* are you?"

He looked at me suspiciously. "Slim Twitchle."

No wonder he'd looked familiar. He'd frequently been a face in our audience as he caught our act before crucifying us with comments like "This band fills a much-needed gap."

"You're telling me this now? Why not when I tackled you? You could have saved us both some trouble."

"I thought you knew me, and you were getting even."

"For what?"

"Oh, you must not have read my last review of your guitar playing."

"What'd you write?"

"That I've heard more interesting cymbal solos. Okay, it's not true, but the truth is always deathly dull. I have readers to entertain—"

That explains why Slim looked nervous the night Richard

was shot; he was worried I would stick my foot so far down his throat we'd be walking home together.

Slim asked, "You mind if I ask you a couple questions?"

"Not if you don't mind that I'm not here." Hoover and I did an about-face.

Slim ran backward alongside us. "Why *did* you tackle me?"

"My brother overheard someone threaten to kill Richard, then I heard you say Fluke was history."

"You mean you knew of the threat beforehand?"

I walked faster. Slim fired questions at me so rapidly my head started to overheat from the strain of keeping my mouth shut.

Finally I burst. "Yes, I knew in advance. Like you did!"

Slim backpedaled around a fire hydrant.

"But I didn't. A friend of Kristin's was supposed to meet me in the Lobster. He never showed. You must've heard me telling my editor that the story about Fluke was history. Why are you still in Cavalry?"

"Let's make a deal. I'll tell you, if you tell me who leaked information about the A.L.F."

"I can't."

"Well then, if I decide to tell you anything, I'll jot it down, wrap it around a rock, and toss it through your hotel window."

"Fair enough. Toss it into the Holiday Inn by noon, my deadline, or I'll be forced to speculate on Kristin's death."

"Meaning?"

"Oh, something like: how Fluke brainwashes teenage girls to burn down research labs."

I worked to remain civil. "Why write stories about Fluke? You said it yourself, we're history."

"You *were* history, but people care about violent death. I've seen it before. If Richard dies, Fluke will be a national story."

In my pocket, my left hand curled in to a fist. "Vulture!"

Half a block ahead, directly in Slim's path, was a *Beacon*

Hill Examiner dispenser. If I could keep him preoccupied, he'd crash into his own garbage bin.

"I'll tell you why I'm staying in Cavalry, but off the record. If you print it, when I'm done with you, your newspaper'll have to pick you up with an ink blotter."

"Deal."

"I'm looking for the psycho who shot Richard."

"Did he have many enemies?"

"Not that I know of. I'm thinking that the target must have been Fluke."

"Nice detective work, young man. You've narrowed down your suspects to all people with good taste in music."

"Your alibi is accepted."

Slim winced. "How are you planning to catch the guy?"

I paused, trying to sound like I knew the answer and was thinking of the clearest way to phrase it.

"Clues."

"Any idea where you'll find 'clues'?"

"Not exactly."

"Then forget it. You'll be searching high and low."

"Just low. That's why I'm here."

Slim skipped sideways and I ran smack into the newspaper dispenser, almost somersaulting over it. In the clear December air, I heard the receding slap, slap of his rubber boots.

Hoover sat at the base of the dispenser as patiently as a stuffed animal. Two women in leather miniskirts and mesh stockings converged on me, offering to engage in acts of leisure.

Not wishing to spend the rest of my life soaking in vats of penicillin, I interrupted them with a dismissing gesture. "No thanks. I'm trying to quit."

* * *

After buying some groceries, Hoover and I went back to our room. I flicked on the light, half expecting battalions of cockroaches to skitter for cover. When I turned on the television, the light dimmed, and someone in the next suite pounded on the wall. I sat in front of the TV, ate Cracker Jacks, and tried to forget I'd known that someone had planned to kill Richard. It was like trying to forget that my head was stuck up my butt.

Should I have warned him? He would have laughed it off. *Should I have stuck closer to him?* Bill was supposed to do that. *Why had he left him alone?*

I was annoyed my thoughts were dwelling so exclusively on what I might have done differently. I had more immediate problems that demanded some attention, namely what I was going to do about earning a living, where I was going to look for Richard's gunman, and what I would do if I actually found him.

A car race was running on the tube. The leader didn't have a rearview mirror. Maybe that was the secret of his success. A commercial came on.

"Listen to that, Hoover. I hope that's great acting. It'd be a shame if that man were really so passionate about motor oil."

Hoover's ears pricked up.

"What's wrong?" He waddled toward the door.

"Want out?"

A sharp knock.

Who knows I'm here? Did somebody find my address in Richard's pocket? Was Richard's gunman stalking A.L.F. members?

Another knock, more persistent.

I heaved my metal suitcase above my head like a caveman's club, and stood to the side of the door. Balancing the suitcase with one hand, I put my other hand on the doorknob, yanked it open, and was amazed.

"It's you!"

"Absolutely correct. Me, herself." Ann sailed through the door, green eyes as large as a night creature's. She was carrying Smuffkins.

"Anyone else?" I leaned into the hallway and looked both ways.

"Just me. Going somewhere?"

"Huh? Oh, no." I set down the suitcase.

Ann placed Smuffkins' blender on the counter.

"May I take your coat?"

"Thank you." Underneath she was wearing a loose black sweater shot through with tiny strands of silver.

I hung her coat on the bent nail next to the door over Hoover's leash.

"I'm glad you're here. I've had just about all I can take of myself."

Ann sat on the couch, her purse nesting in both arms.

"Corky said to bring you Smuffy."

"Thanks. Can I get you anything? There's Coke, and an unopened fifth of Canadian Club left by the previous tenant. Coke, I think, is the better bet, since I don't actually know how to serve Canadian Club."

"No . . . yes, if you're having one."

I poured some into two paper cups and handed her one, then dumped a bag of potato chips into a bowl, took one, and passed the rest to her. Hoover sniffed the air with interest.

"Did you drive here?"

Most of Ann's answer I missed because I was concentrating on the silver strands in her sweater that reflected slightly if hit by light at a certain angle.

". . . a cab and visited Richard," she was saying. "He was groggy, practically asleep, but he says hi."

My eyes traversed the fire escape slashing down the side of the building across the alley.

"Are you headed back to Celtic City?"

She pulled her legs up underneath her and didn't answer until I looked at her.

"I'm not finished here. I came back to cut a deal with Beezil Terrig."

"What deal?"

"We can't have it hanging over our heads that he'll turn

our names over to the police. We'll promise to leave his lab alone if he'll tell us everything he knows, including the source of the leak, and promise he won't reveal any names."

"You can't trust Terrig."

"After burning down his lab, he might not be quick to cross us."

"You want to come with me Thursday when I talk with the Terrig's about Kristin?"

"That might be too late. I think I can reach him today through Lester Gillis."

"You're going to walk right up to Lester and say, 'If you'll play nice, I'll play nice'? Lester may decide it'd be grand entertainment to hurt you."

Ann winked. "I can handle myself around men."

Her courage was enviable, based though it was on a failure to appreciate the difference between a drunken date and a pure evil thug.

"If you were a bookie, Ann, you'd know this. But since you aren't, let me tell you. There is a zero percent chance it'll work. If you ask Lester *not* to reveal A.L.F. names, he'll sense vulnerability and blackmail us to do more than just stay away from Terrig's lab."

Ann smiled without humor.

"What do we have to lose? If Kristin's friend keeps leaking secrets, the A.L.F.'s finished. I'll bluff Lester, tell him we're planning our next raid on Terrig Corporation unless they deal with us. If he already knows *Laurel* is our next target, he'll call my bluff, and I'll know what they know. And we won't walk into a trap."

"You can't be sure. If you want to gamble, why not buy a lottery ticket or eat at a deli?"

"I'll halt the mission the instant anything looks or feels suspicious." Ann took several chips. Hoover sniffed at her tragically. Ann pointed one at me, "Want to work together?"

My answer surprised me. "We have different goals. You want to find out what Lester knows about the A.L.F. and then get ready for the Laurel mission. I want to find Richard's gunman. And I can't ask you to help me, because I don't know what I'm doing."

"Well," she shifted on the couch. "I don't need much help. I'm only going to ask Lester some questions. I'll be fine by myself." Unfortunately, her icy tone implied: "As Mary once said to Joseph: 'Who needs you?'"

"I'll be fine too," I said. "I know a little about detective work from years of television. By the age of twelve I knew how to pick a lock, commit a fairly elaborate bank holdup, and kill people with a variety of sophisticated armaments."

Ann began fiddling with a potato chip, tapping it against her lower lip. Tap-tap-tap. Sigh. Tap-tap-tap. Sigh.

"Any suspects?"

I rearranged loose chips on the coffee table as if preparing to march them off the edge.

"Purple Hair, possibly a good A.L.F. supporter gone bad. Lester Gillis, who suddenly believes his bar is threatened by the Lobster. The guy in the Celica, identity and motive unknown, who also may have been in the neighborhood of the Terrig Lab when it was set on fire. Beezil Terrig, and Kristin's unknown friend. Chas Blat, an ex-con who was right there when Richard was shot."

"How about the guy you tackled in the parking lot?" She patted her thigh and Hoover climbed up, snuggled in, and rested his chin in her lap.

I told her about my encounter with Slim, then I stepped into the kitchenette and poured another Diet Coke.

"Slim chases sensational stories," she said. "Do you think he prods them along?"

"Maybe, but facts bore him. He said 'the truth is dull'. I think what he likes best are the parts he makes up."

Ann stroked Hoover's shoulders. Hoover sniffed and pointed toward the chip bowl.

"I think Hoover is hungry, Clark. He keeps looking at these chips." Hoover tilted his head and furrowed his brow, trying his best to understand English.

"That's probably because you're eating out of his favorite bowl."

Ann grimaced, then laughed and offered Hoover a chip before handing me the bowl. I carried it back to the kitchenette. Hoover cocked his head accusingly.

I poured Ann more Coke. We sipped in silence, relaxed, and talked about food, music, politics, books, and a bad attempt at movies and television. We laughed at ourselves. We'd both lost touch with pop culture since getting involved with the A.L.F. To share memories we had to reach back to *The Right Stuff*, *A Chorus Line,* and the last episode of *M*A*S*H*. We discussed memorable events in Fluke. Some of her perspectives were inspirational, others funny, and all of them fascinating because they were hers.

We avoided our past romances and talked about friends instead. While it was unfortunate that most of our friends were recovering from broken marriages or relationships gone sour, we laughed over the statistical oddity that they were all the wronged parties.

I told her, in detail, of how I'd crushed some of my wrestling opponents. I was aware that I was showing off, and that such macho bragging was silly. *Perhaps I might entertain Ann at a later time by swinging from tree to tree in my leopard skin.* I pondered the notion and found it not wholly without merit.

Several hours had melted away when Ann got up. "This has been great. Sometimes the world goes out of focus when there is no one to share feelings with."

I stood and pushed my hands deep into my pockets.

Ann said, "I'll go with you to hunt for clues, if you'll go with me to talk with Lester."

"Deal." She could have suggested we drive together through hell in a gasoline truck and I'd have agreed.

She opened the door. "Meet you here in one hour. I'm in room 304." She walked out.

I called after her, "I'm falling in love with you, Ann." Although not loud enough for her to hear me. After my divorce, I had given up on love. But here it was, springing up again, a living reminder that love, if not the most powerful force in the world, is at least the most persistent.

13

Through the grimy window I watched the late afternoon lights of Cavalry reflecting off bellies of oceanbound storm clouds.

I called Celtic City and checked my bank account. My balance had all but disappeared due to "service charges," as if the tellers had to take my money for walks or something.

Hoping for some good news, I phoned Dudley. "How'd the stakeout go?"

He yawned. "I spent the morning listening to the car radio for clue number fifteen to the WNN Chain Saw Give-away. No luck. No luck finding the leak, either. No A.L.F. members went in or out. But get this: Mungo stopped by the Terrigs' and stayed for about fifteen minutes. When he left, I followed him to the Lobster. Three cop cars were there. He parked and watched the place for two hours. Nothing happened except . . . who's the bartender who makes Michael Jackson look tough?"

"Mervyn."

"Chas and Mervyn went inside for an hour or so."

"For questioning?"

"Maybe. After they left, they waited for the police to leave, then went back inside."

"Wow. I don't suppose they came out with a shotgun?"

"Couldn't tell you. They were still inside when I left to meet Corky."

"Why would Mungo be watching all this?"

"Good question. Is Bill with you?"

"He's sabotaging a hunt hosted by Mr. Terrig. Why?"

"I thought he could sub for me on the stakeout tomorrow. I have to work at the Aquarium."

"Take tomorrow off. I'm meeting with the Terrigs so I'll be in the neighborhood anyway."

"Thanks." He paused. "You should see your sister in action. She's good."

I hoped for more explanation.

"She's *amazing*. I'm learning a lot. Otherwise I'd help you. You know me. I'd poke a grizzly bear with a short stick if I thought it would help us find the guy who shot Richard. But Corky and I are using the letterhead removed from Terrig Corporation to cancel their suppliers and services, and we're directing their clients to competitors like Schick. It'll be a total mess before Terrig gets wind. Oh, and since we don't know how much has been leaked, Corky moved the Laurel mission up twenty-four hours."

He paused so long I thought the line had gone dead. Then he said, "I don't suppose Corky ever mentioned the reason she dumped me?"

I paused. "My guess is that even eight years ago she had no room for romance in her schedule."

"What should I do? She still thinks I'm teasing when I ask her out."

Dudley Mack is asking me for advice about women. I felt as if I had followed a white rabbit down a burrow into a strange world.

"Any ideas?"

"She's probably afraid of getting involved. Tell her that every moment of life shared with someone who loves you is special. Even if the love doesn't endure."

"That's pretty sentimental."

"I admit, it's probably not advice I'd take."

After we hung up, my next call was to Corky. She was still unhappy I wasn't helping.

"You've got Dudley at your service. That's not a problem, is it?"

"Should it be?"

"Certainly not. It just seems like you go out of your way to avoid him sometimes. I'm not sure why."

"It just never worked out, I guess. Dudley was always busy with his own goals." She stopped talking as if that made everything clear.

"Were his goals a problem?"

"Only in the sense that in college, he had no time for us. His idea of romance was popping his beer can away from my face."

"That was ten years ago, Cork. He's changed. Do you know he carries an old picture of the two of you in his back pocket? I catch him looking at it once in a while."

A long pause. People next door were arguing loudly. Corky was thinking something and wasn't with our conversation anymore. I filled the silence.

"Ten years ago, Cork, I would speed up to smile at a blonde in a Corvette. Now I speed up to read a sign on the truck that says *Jelly Roger Donuts, 7 Locations* to see if one is near me. Dudley's changed, too." After more silence, I said, "Think about it, Cork." She hung up without saying anything. I'm not sure she even heard me.

Twenty minutes later, as I was snapping up the buttons on my jacket, Hoover limped over to the wall, pulled his leash down from the nail, and dragged it over to me.

"Sorry, you look a little swollen. You need rest."

Hoover whined.

I opened the door. Hoover sat, huddled pathetically.

I walked out and closed the door.

I opened it again. Hoover hadn't moved. His head hung low. He was shivering.

I sighed. "Okay."

Hoover bounced energetically up to me, bumping into my leg. *What an actor.*

We picked up Ann and headed uptown, Hoover leading the way, putting his nose to the ground like a miniature bulldozer and hauling Ann away on the leash.

"If we spot a suspect, what's the plan?" Ann asked.

Plan? "Nothing fancy."

"Could you be a tad more specific?"

Is Plan 'A' more specific? Probably not. "How about I chase him until his ankles smoke."

"What'll you do if you catch him? You have no proof he committed a crime."

The cold wind made the Lobster appear to shiver slightly, as though not yet over the recent trauma. "Something will turn up."

"If not?"

"Then I'll be forced to do to him what I did to Slim Twitchle after I tackled him. Be funny until he begs for mercy."

Ann moaned. "That's cruel. Do I have to watch?"

As we entered the parking lot of the Lobster, Hoover's nose tested the air for familiar smells.

I stopped where I'd tackled Slim and tried to visualize what I'd seen that night, bring the picture back in focus: me sitting on Slim's back, Ann perched on his legs, Bill standing in the doorway—and snow, lots of snow. I concentrated harder, trying to see someone leaving in a hurry, or skulking out of the Lobster. Bill came out. No one else.

We circled to the rear of the Lobster. No windows or doors.

"So, Detective Baker, what are we looking for?"

"Telltale cigar butts, torn halves of claim checks, foot-prints, a bent twig or two along the trail. . . ."

"Gotcha. Like traces of lint from an imported caterpillar cloth sold by only one store with one customer." A sudden breeze caught her hair and blew a strand of it across my face. I smelled lilac. She shook her head. "No clues here."

We continued circling the Lobster. Awnings and other sheltered areas were marked by clusters of cigarette butts, Twinkie wrappers, wine bottles, beer cans and other signs of uncivilized life. And every conceivable article of clothing. I wondered how people could possibly have walked home lacking some of the things they'd left behind.

We were back in the parking lot. Something told me the gunman hadn't passed this way. Instinct? Magnum says instinct is what the subconscious sneaks into the memory bank without getting cosigned by the conscious.

What sneaked in? I closed my eyes and focused on the night of the murder.

When I'd tackled Slim, only his car and our van were in the parking lot. The gunman would have had to escape across the lot with the shotgun. Why couldn't I remember seeing him?

"He may have hidden inside the Lobster and ducked out later," I said, silently giving myself credit for having figured something out. It was about time.

We advanced on the Lobster. After a few strides, we stopped dead.

In the window was a hand-lettered sign:

Now Hiring!

Bands—Bartenders—Waitresses

Opening Tonight

"Who could be behind this?" Ann asked. "We know it's not Richard."

"Someone who wants a band other than Fluke." I glanced across the street at the Stagger Back Inn. "Lester won't be happy."

"Unless he's involved."

"That's possible. We shouldn't deal with him until we know."

"Why?"

"The more involved he is, the more dangerous."

"And the more vulnerable."

I'd forgotten that Lester didn't frighten Ann. Once more our priorities clashed. If we learned that Lester had tried to kill Richard to buy the Lobster, Ann would want to use the information to bargain with him. I planned on burying him alive and dancing on his grave.

"How can we find out who took over?"

Ann tapped the sign on the words *Opening Tonight*. "Why don't we stop by tonight and have a look around Richard's office."

My mind's eye saw Richard's blood on the wall. "Sure," I said. *Let's keep dancing in the minefield.*

Heading in the direction from which darkness was descending, Ann and I took Hoover back to his doctor for a follow-up visit.

While waiting at Dr. Dean's kitchen table, Ann opened Wednesday's *Examiner* and started laughing. She handed me the paper—another Twitchle article, this one with a photo of me. I wanted to believe it had been electronically altered.

I looked as if I'd spent a week doing sit-ups under parked cars. My eyes seemed impossible without intoxication, drug use, lack of sleep, or psychopathy. The tone of the article matched the photo—I was obsessed with chasing an unknown assailant, and all citizens in the county should watch out for me driving through their neighborhood shooting a gun out the window.

I tossed the paper on the floor where it landed like a half-collapsed tent. Ann picked it up, folded it so my photo was on top, and started laughing again.

For the next few minutes, every time I made eye contact with her, she laughed hysterically. I decided this constituted with her, she laughed hysterically. I decided this constituted excessive mirth at my expense.

"It's not that funny."

"You're right, it's not." Then she looked at me and slid off into hysterics again.

My eyes teared as I choked out again that it wasn't that funny.

Dr. Dean came out of the examining room.

"He's doing pretty well, but there is some swelling. You mind leaving him with me for observation?"

We said a long good-bye to Hoover. Outside, Ann and I got into an old Dodge she'd borrowed. Possibly metallic brown at one time, it was now the color of mustard gone bad. She drove.

The parking lot of the Lobster was full. We circled the block to look for a spot and got stuck in traffic by a church. A glass case containing white letters on a black background listed the topics of the next sermon (essentially, all the things people like to do). A limousine pulled out in front of us with JUST MARRIED painted on the trunk. Traffic started to move.

"So, what spoiled your marriage, Clark?" Ann asked.

"It hit an underwater stump and sunk. There's a spot." To my relief, Ann shifted her attention to parallel parking on ice.

I held onto my baseball cap as the wind propelled us toward the Lobster. The GRAND OPENING sign hung a little askew. At the door, Chas greeted us in a tuxedo. He seemed to have gained at least five pounds since I'd last seen him.

"Great to see you," he said. "Thanks for coming."

I handed him the five-dollar cover charge. He waved it away as if fighting off a swarm of bees.

I wanted to ask him who had reopened the Lobster, and why Fluke hadn't been invited to audition, but the next group of people arrived at the door, and besides, his scars reminded me that he was an ex-con and no stranger to violence.

Inside was the fevered excitement one expects only at championship heavyweight fights. People were three deep at the bar and booths lining the walls were packed. On the dance floor, if my math was correct, 3.6 whomptillion people were frantically dancing to the beat of Geezer Fever. Geezer's youngest member was over seventy. Their lead singer had skin like leather, blue eyes buried in a mess of laugh lines, and shocks of white hair pointing every which way. Einstein enjoying a bad hair day.

Ann headed for the stage. I headed for the bar until I recognized a group of teenagers from the night Richard was shot. I hovered on the fringe of their conversation.

"Heard about the shooting?" said a girl.

"Yeah. Cool, huh?" replied her friend. "Maybe he'll strike again."

Throughout the evening I divided my time between eavesdropping and keeping an eye on Ann. At ten minutes to midnight she began lounging near the EMPLOYEES ONLY door. Chas was standing near the bar watching her. He waved his hand, conjured up a Snickers bar, and caressed it twice before unwrapping it the way one undresses a lover for the first time. When Ann slipped into the back, Chas was so surprised he almost stopped chewing. He glanced at his watch, loosened his collar, walked to the door, and wedged through the doorway.

My stomach went on spin cycle.

I moved to the door, eased through, stopped and listened— nothing, I stalked down the hallway and rounded a corner into a narrower, darker corridor. I heard a noise—Ann's voice from Richard's office. I peered around the doorway into the office.

Chas, his back to me, was holding Ann's hands away from a brass letter opener lying between them on the desk. Ann tugged at her hands as though unable to understand why they did not move as she wished.

Adrenaline tore through my veins.

I began sneaking up behind Chas, step by step.

Ann glanced up and saw me. Her eyes gaped, giving away my presence, but she recovered her poise and forced her eyes back down. Her action was too deliberate.

Chas stood, turned, and leaned forward like a mountainous cresting wave about to break. My first instinct was to kneel and pray. Instead, head down, I plowed straight into him. Before I could blink, he'd seized both Ann's head and mine, like footballs, one under each powerful arm—tight enough to let me know that if he wanted to, he could compress my head into a dumpling with just one flex of his biceps.

Many wrestling opponents had fashioned me into that position and I had escaped. All I had to do was grab Chas with my legs and twist hard until he lost balance. But I was staring directly at bloodstains and shotgun pellets in the splintered wall and something rustled in the back of my mind like a wild thing hiding in the bushes, but it was crouching so still I couldn't make it out.

Abruptly, Chas released us. "Now, tell me," he said, moving between me and the door, thereby thwarting my first plan. "What do you think you're doing?"

Ann spoke first, stretching her neck to loosen it.

"We figure whoever reopened the Lobster shot Richard to get it."

The flesh around Chas's scars grew whiter.

"I reopened the bar. But I didn't shoot Richard—"

"Sure," I muttered. I had not wanted it to sound as doubtful as it did.

"You saying you don't believe me?"

"Not at all." *Why would I choose those as my last words?*

"Why did you attack me?"

"Point one," I said, "you're an ex-con for reasons unknown. Two, you had a motive—financial gain from the bar. Three, you had the best opportunity. You were first to reach Richard, and you might have gone to the hospital to ensure he didn't tell us anything. Four, when Richard was shot, I was outside in the parking lot. No one ran past me with a shotgun, but you could have hidden the shotgun inside and removed it later. Dudley saw you return after the cops left."

Chas put his hands to his head and squeezed lightly, as if testing a cantaloupe for ripeness. Suddenly I knew the significance of the pellets in the wall. Their height. "And five," I said, "Richard was shot in the face and the chest. The wall behind him was splintered knee-high. There was only one blast, which means it was fired downward by someone very tall. Like you."

"Keep it up," Chas sighed heavily, "and I'll find my own self guilty. It's true I reopened the club illegally, but only until I earned enough money to give Richard all the hospital care he needs, and to pay the Lobster's mortgage. That's why I hired the Geezers. To save money." He threw himself onto the couch.

Ann asked, "Doesn't Richard have health insurance?"

"No. But in about a week I should be able to pay his bills." Chas squirmed around on the couch, unable to find a position that fit. "Unless, that is, you have me arrested—"

"Chas!" Mervyn appeared in the doorway, ashen. "Two cops are outside. They say they want to talk to you."

"Damn!" Chas said, fingering a scar on his forehead. "They wanted this crime scene secured, but they usually ignore this side of town. Lester knows I'm on probation, he must have called them." His eyes darted around the room. No windows. No closets. "Looks like this was a bad mistake."

"Maybe you can escape," Mervyn whispered. He glanced at Ann and me, his eyes pleading as he backed out the door and closed it. "I think he's in the kitchen, officers."

"Who's in there?"

"Just two of the band members."

Chas crouched behind the desk, which hid only part of him. I stood in front of the desk, hoping to conceal the rest of him, but it was futile.

A slight brushing noise against the door froze me. As the

handle turned, Ann moved in front of me and, to my wonderment, pushed me backward onto the desk and dove on top of me.

CRASH! The door burst wide open.

A deep male voice stammered, "Wha . . . excuse me, sorry . . ." Then he sighed with annoyance and shut the door. Through the door, I heard him say, "I'll check the storage room. Meet you in the kitchen."

Chas rose. "Thanks."

I vaulted to the door and looked both ways. "All clear."

Chas's huge forehead puckered in puzzlement, "That was really nice of you guys. Why'd you do it?"

"Go!" I said.

Chas waited for an answer. I tried pulling him toward the door, but I might as well have tried pulling the door toward him.

Ann answered: "We helped you because it means now you owe us. We like that trait in a person."

Chas smiled and left, then Ann and I walked through the lounge, outside, and across the parking lot.

"That was quick thinking," I said.

"Thanks."

I opened the car door on the driver's side. Ann got in and slid across the seat, inviting me to drive. I got in and twisted the key. The engine shuddered in the cold, then turned over.

"Why did Chas grab you?"

"I guess he didn't like me going through Richard's desk. When he barged in on me I panicked and grabbed a letter opener. Huge mistake, solidly in my all-time top ten. But then I looked up and like a miracle, you appeared in the doorway."

"I'm glad Chas didn't want to hurt us. I'd prefer to be dropped from a great height onto rotating helicopter blades."

The Dodge plowed through fast-falling snow, the windshield wipers clicking and clacking to different beats.

"Since we helped Chas escape," Ann said, "I gather neither of us believe he shot Richard."

Suddenly I realized what poor judgement I'd used. I had helped Chas because I liked him. As simple as that. But how many times had I watched a television news reporter interviewing the neighbors of a mass murderer: "I can't believe he did it." "He was such a nice man."

"I figure there's no way Chas could have shot Richard."

"Really?" Hope was in her voice.

"No time. He never stopped eating."

Ann punched my shoulder. "He was involved somehow. Lester left a message for him on Richard's answering machine, 'Do exactly as I told you, or I won't protect your friends in the A.L.F.'"

I stopped at a red light. "How's that possible? Chas isn't an A.L.F. member."

"Maybe he was."

"Doubtful. Even in disguise Chas would've been as inconspicuous as Smuffy on a slice of angel-food."

Ann pointed ahead. The light had turned green and vehicles behind us were sliding past.

"So why does Lester think Chas cares about the A.L.F.?"

"Maybe it's 'blackmailer versus blackmailer'. When Mungo saw Chas in the Lobster, he reacted as if he'd swallowed a bottle cap. Maybe Chas has something on him." I stopped at a stop sign a block from the Suite Night. "I'll ask Chas tomorrow. Assuming I can find him."

"Maybe Richard was shot because he was protecting the A.L.F. and he *wouldn't* be blackmailed."

The thought that Richard was shot while protecting us jarred me. I slammed the Dodge into a random gear and we went kangarooing down the block, coming to a final bounce and stop in front of the Suite Night.

Ann and I went past the sleeping desk clerk, then upstairs. After I said good-night, I watched Ann go into her room and heard the click of her lock.

As I approached my room, I noticed a key in the lock. I squatted and examined it, then pulled it out. It looked like a key to another room—maybe someone had gotten confused. I listened for a minute before unlocking the door. Feeling less fearful than paranoid, I reached in with my right hand, switched on the light, and pushed the door gently. Except for snow brushing against the window, the room stood silent. So silent I imagined hearing Smuffy communicating with unseen spiders moving in dark corners.

I took one step inside.

I heard a faint swoosh behind me.

Later I was able to recall only jagged pieces of consciousness.

The sound of something going crunch on my head.

The sight of my keys leaving my hand, arcing away.

The taste of linoleum.

But I don't remember closing my eyelids and going nighty-night.

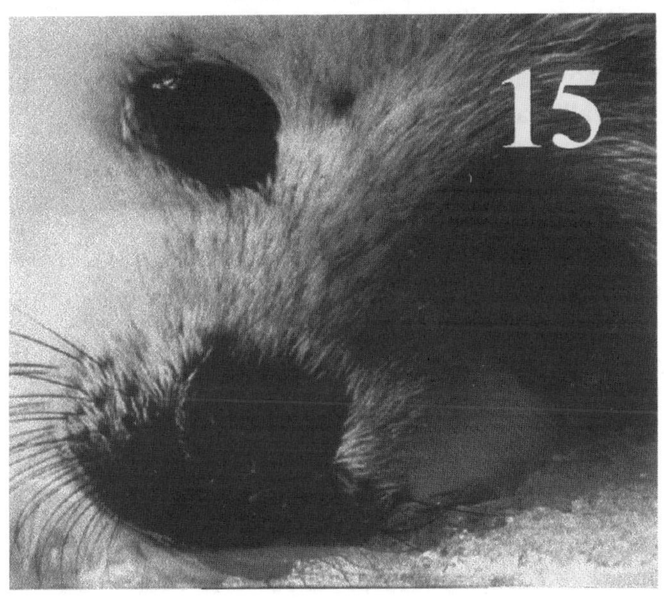

Fluke was playing basketball against Mungo, Lester, Beezil, Slim, and Purple Hair. Time was running out when I took a no-look behind-the-back pass from Ann. At the final buzzer, as I arced away the game-deciding shot, a crunching elbow to the head knocked me down. The ball clanked off the rim.

I woke up depressed.

The floor had leeched the warmth from my body. I breathed deeply, inched my arms under me, and pushed myself up onto my hands and knees, like a sailor washed ashore after a shipwreck.

My awareness came in stages. *Was I still in a basketball arena?* No. I was in the Suite Night Hotel. *Did I run into something?* Long, careful thought. *No.* The back of my head hurts. *What then?* Aha. Somebody hit me from behind. Now I was clear-headed enough to know I should be alarmed. Someone could be standing over me with an Uzi machine gun. Yet, I could muster up only a mild concern.

I fought my way to a cross-legged sitting position and

checked my watch. Five a.m. I'd been sleeping facedown on the floor nearly three hours. I felt my pockets: the outline of my wallet and the key I'd found in the door.

Getting up was a mistake. My head spun and I sat down backward. The sudden movement set pain whirring.

After several minutes, I wobbled up and turned on the light. The room looked as if someone had picked it up and shaken it. The bed, the chair, and the television were tipped over. Drawers stuck out from the teetering dresser like tongues trying to tell me something. Underwear, socks, and T-shirts were strewn everywhere. The mattress was slit open and stuffing pulled out. Even the door to the refrigerator was open.

At first I figured my ex-wife had sent her lawyer over for another round. Then I checked my wallet. Thirty-four dollars. Skidmark Murphy would never have left cash behind.

With the uncertainty of a baby's first steps, I walked to Ann's door and knocked.

She wore a filmy flesh-colored nightgown with white overtones, its neckline showing some freckles at her throat.

"Good morning. What happened to you?"

"Got clubbed like a baby seal. Someone ransacked—"

Ann pushed past me. I wobbled after her to my room, where she already was looking around at the chaos. The room hadn't been burglarized; it had been searched. And the ransacker hadn't found what he'd been looking for, unless he found it in the very *last* place he thought to look, which seemed improbable, except that it happens to me a lot.

"No thief did this," I said.

"Who then?"

I thumbed the money in my wallet. "Don't know, but in this neighborhood, thirty-four dollars would be a nice haul. Maybe Richard's gunman?"

"Sure. He might've been looking for something he thought Richard had, and thinks you now have."

"Or he might be trying to scare us off."

"Or perhaps staying two days in this neighborhood, without being savagely violated, is simply pushing the odds."

I headed for the fridge.

"Breakfast?"

"Please. I'm famished."

"It won't be fancy. I have a bachelor's cooking skills—throw food at the stove, eat it, then clean up."

"I'll help."

Ann held the wastebasket as I took from the refrigerator all the food the intruder might have touched—bread in aluminum foil even though it didn't appear to have been tampered with, a jar of pickles with a screw-on top, several other items which, like every other product currently sold in the United States including Drano, were marked "Low Cholesterol."

All that remained was an unopened box of pancake mix and a Weight Watchers frozen entree. Since the Weight Watchers entree was a convenient product that came right out of the box with most of the food already eaten for you, we settled on pancakes.

The telephone rang.

"You still looking for a white Celica?"

"You've seen it?"

"There still a reward?"

"Absolutely. Who is this?"

"Sam Johnson. Johnson's Auto Repair. How much?"

"Two tickets to the Patriots-Steelers playoff game. Forty-eight yard line."

"No kidding? Thing is, I don't know whose it is, I've only seen it, near the hospital, coming and going. I'm a big Patriots fan."

"I'll drop the tickets off today."

"I'll be waiting."

"I'm going to visit Richard," I said as we finished breakfast. "He might know whether he has anything worth killing for. Then I'll drop off the football tickets and scout around for the Celica. Care to join me?"

"Can't. I'm not certain if your getting clubbed is related to the Laurel mission, but I need to call every A.L.F. member and find out if anything else suspicious happened last night. If we're under attack, the mission goes on hold."

"But if the mission is delayed, the rabbits will die."

"It won't be an easy decision. Give Richard my best. I'll catch up with you later." The shadows of her nightgown shimmered and dissolved as she moved through the doorway.

* * *

I called Mervyn at the Lobster.

"Remember the night Richard was shot? You talked with a reporter in a brown leather coat."

"Slim? Sure. Mostly chitchat. Plus one question he knew I wouldn't answer: if I would point out anyone in the A.L.F. Said he was waiting for an A.L.F. member."

"Anything else?"

"He'd just come from the Stagger Back Inn. City inspectors are cracking down hard there. Code violations. Gillis has been fighting city hall and losing. Now he's got money problems and he's drinking again."

"So that's why suddenly he's uptight about competition. Any inspectors been digging around the Lobster?"

"No."

"I wonder what made them go after the Stagger Back, aside from the fact that it looks less like a lounge than an upholstered sewer?"

Mervyn's voice dropped to a whisper. "You know Petey, the waitress? She tipped them off. Anonymously."

"How'd she know about code violations?"

"Petey dated Mungo a couple of times, until he slapped her once. Lester was right there and joked, 'What do you tell a woman with two black eyes?' He paused. 'Nothing. You already told her twice.' Petey was so mad she called the city and told them Lester'd rewired the place without a permit.

Turned out it was all to code because he was an electronics expert in the army and knew what he was doing, but the city made him tear it out anyway."

"Did Lester ever find out that Petey turned him in?"

"Doubt it. She's still breathing."

"Mervyn, thanks. I'll see you later."

"Whatever you're doing, Clark, be careful."

Next I looked up Blat in the phone book and found only one, Edith. I called her.

"Do you know Chas Blat?"

"Yes, sir, I do."

"May I talk with you about Chas?"

"Yes, sir, you may."

I took a taxi. Edith was a grand old lady, dressed formally although she didn't appear to be going anywhere. She offered me tea and finger cakes, and shared fond memories of her great-nephew Chas. She'd moved out of Cavalry with her husband, then returned last year after he died. Her information about Chas ended when he was three, joyously splashing through puddles, walking with her husband and their basset. Every memory Edith shared was tied intimately to a memory of her husband. She was old and lonely, and I stayed an hour. I managed to say good-bye without promising to come back and visit. Maybe I would anyway.

The hospital's receptionist scolded me for not bringing Hoover.

The nurse behind the desk on Richard's floor wore a badge that said SUPERVISOR.

"Richard Tipton," I said.

"Go ahead, he already has a visitor."

I hadn't seen the van in the parking lot. *Who else can it be?*

But Richard was alone, propped up asleep against pillows, feeding off five-percent dextrose. He was hooked to a monitor that transformed impulses into waveforms that looked as if they belonged on his sound-sampling keyboard oscilloscope. I tiptoed past his bed and cracked one of the windows open to a thin stream of frigid December air.

I sat and held his hand, but he was too deep in sleep or too drugged to acknowledge me. When I lowered his hand back onto the bed, I nearly leapt up out of my chair. Curled on the sky-blue sheet was a four-inch strand of purple hair.

I went back to the nurses' station. "Who was the other visitor?"

An alarm went off. The supervisor looked at her console, shot me a glance, then ran off towards Richard's room. I followed.

The room filled with doctors and nurses. Commands were barked, syringes were pumped. I stood in the middle like some startled animal until a nurse ushered me out.

I paced, occasionally exchanging glances with an elderly gentleman who kept checking his watch, both of us wired to detonate. I wanted to comfort him, share his grief, but I didn't. Didn't want to lose my focus on Richard. As if it mattered.

A face appeared in front of mine—the nurse.

"What happened?" I asked.

"We're not sure. His heart almost stopped."

"Is he okay now?"

"Adrenaline brought him back. He regained consciousness for a few minutes, then fell asleep. You'll probably be able to see him tomorrow."

"Who visited him before I did?"

She looked at me like I'd wandered down the hall from the Head-trauma wing.

"We don't give out that kind of information, sir."

I'm not especially good at confrontation. I'm better at trying to please and then resenting it. She pointed her finger to the door. Under my breath, I ranted and raved. Fortunately for her, I am one of those odd Americans who doesn't always carry a loaded handgun, so she was able to sneer at my ranting with impunity.

Outside, as I passed the Paul Revere fountain, I gazed down at my reflection. My eyes were deep black holes and I appeared to have sharper cheekbones than I really did.

I couldn't guard the hospital day and night. I needed to track down Purple Hair.

Pinned on Sam Johnson's office wall were three Patriot posters. He was elated with the playoff tickets.

"Yeah, I saw the kid in the Toyota this morning. This time I noticed his hair. Odd color. It seemed to change shades as he drove by."

"Thanks, Sam. Go Patriots!"

I spent an hour walking streets around Johnson's. No white Celica. Getting cold, I gave up and headed home, down Washington Street.

At Firebone's Used Cars, I stopped. There, under frozen crossing stringers of yellow, white, and red plastic pennants, amongst cars ranging from old VW's to full-sized vans, was a white Celica with a fresh metallic scar carved along the rear fender. *Why would he park here?* Maybe he worried I'd seen his license plate and reported a hit-and-run. When the police came to arrest him, he'd declare the car had been stolen.

Reality knocked me flat. I had no proof Purple Hair intentionally ran me off the road. Nor did I have a motive. I peered inside the Celica, looking for clues. From behind me, I heard a voice, "Hey! You! Looking for trouble?"

I was.

In the cold Atlantic wind his purple hair danced wildly beneath carnivorous eyes you'd expect to see in the jungle, casing you from behind a clump of foliage.

"Kiss your ass good-bye!"

Not even if I could. "What's the problem here?"

"You killed my girlfriend!"

Bill was right, Purple Hair had been an A.L.F. member. I'd spotted his car the night Kristin died. She'd probably been expecting him to pick her up.

"Who are you?"

"Brett Tarbatz." He moved closer. "Don't bother trying to remember. You won't remember your own name after I kick your spine out the top of your head."

He was at least twenty pounds heavier than me, about ten years younger, and pumped with anger. I was in trouble. I'd recently needed Ann's help to get the best of an aging newspaper reporter. I remembered something the TV detective Simon once said, "Talk tough enough and it's as good as landing the first punch."

I tried to look sadistic. "Don't come even a half step closer unless you want your tongue braided!" *Sheesh! That sounds like something girls do at slumber parties. I'll have to work on my threats.*

As Brett shook his head in disbelief, I made a fist and hit him square on his beefy nose. He slipped, bounced off his car, and went down like a Caucasian heavyweight.

I hoped he'd stay down, but I knew from his eyes he was going to spring at me. As he was coming to a crouch, I swung. He twisted sideways, making me miss. Momentum carried my body too close to his and he smashed his meaty fist just under my lowest rib the way a wrecking crew with a swinging ball smashes buildings. I crumbled.

I looked up from the lotus position.

Brett grabbed me by the throat and I popped him in the face. No weight behind it, just arm. Pain shot through my shoulder when I connected. He fell on his butt on the pavement.

I stood, but my knees started to give way. When I tried to lock them, I wavered like a newborn colt.

Brett rose more quickly than I expected, wiped blood from his nose and started toward me. I faced him, on the balls of my feet. We were both circling, the distance between us just longer than a kick. Moving in, he hit me with a left cross. Quick to swing, he was slow to get ready. He swung and missed. This time, before he readied, I moved in, hit him hard twice in the gut and twice in his face.

He went down on one knee.

I leaned back on the hood of the car, letting life drain back into me.

"Why do you blame me?"

"I can't breathe." His croaking wheeze corroborated his statement. "We believed in the A.L.F. We knew we could go to jail. No one told us we could die."

"The A.L.F. targets only equipment like decapitators and electrode implanters. Not buildings we aren't certain are free of all life. Her death, though tragic, was her own fault. You can't blame the A.L.F."

"Her father and I blame you."

"So *you* leaked the A.L.F.'s secrets to Beezil!"

"Damned right!" A bull pawing dust couldn't have looked more belligerent. "Anything to keep another innocent girl from dying. I was going to tell the press. Told Mr. Twitchle to meet me at the Lobster."

"Why'd you jump onto the stage?"

"I was angry and wanted to give Slim a negative story to print about Fluke."

I raised my voice. "Did you shoot Richard?"

"I hate you all! I wanted to kill you. I followed you, ran you off the road, sneaked poison into the hospital—"

Poison! I ran.

Inside the hospital, I took the stairs two at a time. The nurse on Richard's floor told me I couldn't go into Richard's room. I ignored her, but she cut me off, then touched the welt on my cheek. "Dear God, those are fresh welts. What kind of trouble do you keep getting into? Come with me."

"I'm okay. I need to know if a visitor could have caused Richard's heart to falter by poisoning his dextrose?"

"No one would do that," she started to turn but saw the look in my eyes and halted as suddenly as if I'd stepped from behind a bush and grabbed her arm.

"Is it possible?" I asked.

"The monitor alerts us of all tampering."

"Tampering has happened before?"

Her expression softened. "Men have tried to add alcohol to their own bags."

I left the hospital and cut through George's Cemetery where a strong cold wind brought ice crashing down from tree branches.

Brett and the Toyota were gone.

As my adrenaline subsided I began to feel the full measure of the damage Brett had inflicted. In my head. My neck. My lower back. My hands. There was one spot below my left eye that felt okay, but pretty much everything else hurt.

I headed for the Suite Night. My right knee throbbing in time with the beating of my heart, my aching muscles stiffening with the cold, soon I was lurching like Boris Karloff in one of his cheaper movies.

A police car passed me, driven by the same boneless policeman who'd interrogated me in the hospital. I averted my eyes, but then realized he wouldn't notice me; with a ripped jacket, blood on my chin, and tears in my eyes, I was not very conspicuous in this part of town.

Not that my appearance went entirely unnoticed. When I crossed the street in front of a family in a stopped minivan, they synchronously locked the doors, a drill they had obviously practiced before leaving home.

At my room I missed being greeted by Hoover's happy face. I leaned on the counter and watched Smuffkins stretching her legs on the glass wall of the food processor, reaching out, trying to make contact with the world. Conveying by means of body language the concept of "Please oh PLEASE pay attention to me . . ." And I know precisely why you're reaching out, Smuffy! You're saying, "Please look at me! I'm so unique! So irreplaceable! So alone! Look at me and love me!" For my money, she is far better at this kind of silent communication than those people called "mimes."

I called Corky and asked her to have someone watch Richard's hospital room.

"Done."

I told her I'd found the leak.

"I'll ask around, try to learn more about Brett," she said, "and I'll pull any operative he's worked with off the Laurel mission. But didn't Chas throw him out of the Lobster that night?"

"Literally."

"Then how could he have shot Richard?"

"I'm not sure."

After I said good-bye, I went to the cupboard. My box of Cracker Jacks had teeth marks where something had beaten me to it, so I got an Eskimo Whip from the fridge instead. Then I called Dudley.

"Caught anyone?" he asked.

I told him of my encounter with Brett.

"You're getting good at this detective stuff. Maybe there's a career in it for you."

"I already broke the first rule."

"What's that?"

"You're supposed to have a client."

"Ah yes. In that case, while you're mastering the rules, you might try counseling. Thanks to your advice, I opened my heart to Corky—"

I advised that?

"—and told her that I still liked her, that I wanted to start again, slowly, and was hoping she'd let me buy her a modest dinner, and perhaps let me escort her to a small European country."

"What'd she say?"

"We talked for hours about our convictions and how they've handicapped our relationships. She said she'd become self-contained after her, um, your father's death. She used to be proud she didn't need anyone for emotional support, that she wasn't vulnerable."

"You can't get hurt that way." Like her, I believed wanting something of other people was selfish and having them want something of me would ultimately lead to my disappointing them. So I just stayed away from people. The truth is that I have been more an observer than human being, and my heart has always served my head. Poorly.

"I told her how I feel when I'm not with her. It's like I'm just killing time."

That's touching. Now, if you'll excuse me, I have to put my finger down my throat. "Why Corky? Is it because she's the only girl not interested in you?"

There was a long pause. Maybe I'd overstepped my boundary as a friend, or maybe as a protective brother.

I clung to the image of Corky the year Dad died. She was twelve and her bed was covered with furry pink and green stuffed animals. The next year, posters of nearly naked sweaty rock stars hung on the walls, but I considered it a passing fad.

"Fair question," Dudley said. "Detective work has made you spunky. I love her commitment and dedication. She loves things based on their worth, not their appearance." He paused. "I want to make sure nothing bad ever happens to her."

"Sorry, Dudley. Sorry I doubted you."

"No problem. Happens all the time."

* * *

Hoover slept all the way home from Dr. Dean's office. At the Suite Night he came to life, staggered to his feet and wandered around, sniffing and tottering like a little old four-legged man. I told him it was terrific having him back. He wagged his tail, lapped at his water bowl as if he hadn't drunk in days, then went back to sleep.

"What's that you're humming?" Ann asked.

"Humming? Was I?" Bad omen. Only two kinds of people hum unconsciously, those who are falling in love, and those who argue with buses.

"Do you think we can find Brett before the mission tomorrow night?" she asked.

I handed her a Coke.

"Can't count on it, but we need to know what he leaked. That's one reason I'm keeping my appointment with the Terrigs."

She stared at me, her index finger poised to open her Coke as if she were holding a pose for a painter.

"You're still going to go see Beezil after he hired Lester to hurt you? Wouldn't it be easier to let me beat you up right here, save you the drive?"

"We owe it to Kristin. Besides, I have a plan. Want to come?"

"Sure, I'll tag along. It'll give me the opportunity to see if my first-aid kit is complete and in order." She opened the cup-board. "You're out of food."

"I'll run over to the Quick Mart." Hoover and I got up, both of us grunting a little.

The phone rang.

"Hello?" I heard the click of someone hanging up. Even a card-carrying optimist would expect nothing good from that.

Hoover waddled after me to the door. I petted him on the head and told him to stay and protect Ann. It was easier than telling Ann that I was worried.

At the Quick Mart I found Cracker Jacks, Eskimo Whips, jam, peanut butter, and bread. I piled them on the checkout counter next to a display of water pistols: "On sale. Replicas of the authentic Luger." I took one.

Back at the Suite Night the door to my room was cracked open. Off to the side, I set down my groceries and listened for sounds. It was too quiet. A pulse in my throat started kicking. I could smell the strange briny smell of radiator steam. I leaned toward the crack in the doorway.

My eye was greeted by a .45-caliber pistol.

"Over there." Mungo waved me to the side of the room where Ann sat in the ratty chair. His gun muzzle made impatient arcs, circling, pointing one moment at my chest, the next at my face. I heard growling—Hoover was trapped in the bathroom.

"See this gun?" Mungo's eyes were bloodshot and he smelled of alcohol.

"How can I miss it? You're pointing it at me. Why?" Hoover began frantically scratching at the bathroom door.

"Lester says never to trust fools who believe dumb animals should be treated as good as pets." He raised his eyebrows as if to say, "Understand?" Evidently I didn't look convinced because he poked my chest with the gun barrel and cocked the hammer.

I don't know guns, but the one burrowing into my chest didn't seem to have a silencer.

"My neighbors will hear the shot."

He laughed. "And run to lock their doors." He used the gun to push me away, then he leered at Ann, bringing tongue and eyebrows into play. I almost forgot he had the gun and went at him. Almost.

He staggered around the couch and stopped in front of Ann.

With exaggerated slow motion he placed his hand on her cheek and stroked it, turning his head so he could watch my reaction as his huge hand felt its way down her neckline.

A low growl came from the back of her throat, but she didn't move.

I edged sideways, angling, trying to get closer.

The gun muzzle followed me like an empty eye socket. His finger was on the trigger and he didn't seem to be paying close attention to whether or not he was squeezing.

Hoover barked. Mungo glared at the bathroom door, but his gun stayed trained on me, daring me to move.

"Unless you want the A.L.F.'s next target to be warned, you gotta do two things. Shut down the Lobster—"

"Don't worry," I said. "Chas opened the Lobster for only a few days."

"Only a fool who doesn't know Blat would believe that. You also gotta return all the dogs you stole from Terrig's lab."

"Can't do that."

"Remember what happened to Tipton?"

He cracked the back of his hand across my face, catching me off balance and knocking me down hard onto the cold linoleum. I started to get up, but he shook his head. I felt like a dog being trained to stay.

"You even think about moving, your brains'll fly out the back of your head."

I stayed. I prepared to roll over, sit up, and beg if need be. My internal reactions collided. Anger, and beneath that, humiliation. But neither was making much headway against the fear of having my brain become a Rorschach inkblot test on the wall behind me.

Mungo turned to go, saw Smuffkins reaching out her arms toward him and did a double take, whipping his head without realizing his proximity to the doorjamb. This slight misjudgment made a sound like a ripe melon dropping onto the pavement. A very satisfying sound, indeed. He cursed and stumbled out the door.

Ann and I stared numbly at the open door for several seconds before letting out an intertwined sigh. I helped her out of the chair.

"Did he hurt you?"

"No. What a worm. It's a shame that things have learned to walk that ought to crawl." She looked at Smuffy. "No offense. You sure startled him."

"Mungo will see Smuffy in his nightmares."

I let Hoover out of the bathroom. He whooped and moaned and tried squirming into my jacket.

"Mungo actually implied he and Lester shot Richard for Mr. Terrig," Ann said. "Does he think they're above the law?"

"Could be. Terrig Corporation dominates so much of the economic life here—jobs, taxes. It wouldn't surprise me if it wields power over local authorities."

Ann's expression changed with an unreadable emotion. "How did Mungo find us?"

"He might have tailed me, or found me by whatever means he found me in Chez Beagle." *Or, with the way my luck's been running, he's my secret Santa.*

"Maybe Lester's boys planted a bug on your van," Ann said. "Since they obviously know we're here, I'd say we can thank them for the ransacking?"

"That doesn't seem like Lester's style, though. If he wanted anything I had, I believe he'd just beat me to a jelly and make me give it to him."

"Who then?"

I tried to think of other candidates. But after having been slapped by Mungo, I had to concentrate hard just to keep my eyes from crossing.

Ann said, "Do you think Lester really knows Laurel is our next target?"

"Hard to say. Mungo could be bluffing."

She smoothed her dress with a nervous, patting motion.

"Our plan was to send a scout. He was going to park in front of Laurel, march around for a few minutes, then knock on the door and ask to use a phone. If the Laurel guard called the cops, they'd find nothing, and the mission would never start. But now it seems Lester and his thugs might set up an ambush and make Laurel seem vulnerable until we're all trapped inside."

I stared out the window at the snow sifting down in the checkerboard light from other tenement windows.

"What if I break in through a rear door and get the drop on the guard?" I pulled my gaze back to a closer point of focus and watched Ann's reflection.

"Too risky. There's got to be a better way." But her voice died at the end as if she were giving the idea more thought.

Snow melted on the window and speckled the room with the watery shadows of beads tracking down the glass. I felt those beads crawling over me.

17

I drove the old-mustard Dodge through winding roads.

"If Beezil hired someone to shoot Richard the day after Kristin's death," I said, "it might've been someone already working for him."

"Let's look for a tall butler," Ann said.

We cruised beyond the Terrigs' home, U-turned, and approached it from the other direction. The alabaster-white mansion would have been impressive as a wing of the Taj Mahal. I parked in the shadows of a white marble fence. We got out and walked through the main gate. Somewhere nearby, a dog barked.

Ann strolled next to me, our shoulders nearly touching. I imagined how nice it would be to hold her hand.

A marble fountain of what looked like an angel peeing stood near the front patio. I punched the bronze button by the door. The chimes were still bonging when a butler appeared and crinkled up his nose.

"What can I do for you?" He used the same tone of voice he would have used to say, "What the hell do you want?"

"We have an appointment with Mr. and Mrs. Terrig."

He sniffed very loudly when he offered to take my baseball cap. I told him I didn't trust him with it.

He ushered us into the living room, its walls shaded in quiet colors and enriched with enormous paintings. The ceilings were rimmed with moldings crafted with skills unsummoned for generations. Oriental carpets, warm woods, and polished brass basked in the soft glow of recessed lighting.

Mrs. Terrig stood in the middle of the room wearing multiple strands of pearls and a blue velvet gown. She didn't look as pale as she had on television, maybe because she was wearing enough makeup to paint the side of a barn. She was cradling a toy poodle.

"Nice to meet you, Mrs. Terrig," I said. "This is Ann Berlin. I'm Clark Baker."

"Welcome. This is Mitzi." Mrs. Terrig exchanged glances with the poodle, then gave us the best smile she could manage without moving the muscles around her eyes. A well-bred lady of uncertain age, certain surgery. "Mitzi is good-natured." She leaned forward so I could scratch Mitzi's ear. Mitzi yawned.

"We're terribly sorry about Kristin's death," I said.

"A sad, sad loss. We're about to enjoy dessert." Death and dessert sharing equally in her thoughts, she turned and walked down the hallway as if she expected us to follow her, which we did; across a hand-painted tile floor, past formal portraits of stern-looking Terrigs in charcoal suits and ruffled shirts, up a marble staircase with a window that looked over a twenty-acre yard, and into a dining room lit by three gold candelabras on an immense dining table.

Beezil Terrig sat at the far end wearing a dark suit and a dirty look. Something seemed to be gnawing at him. *What do they say? Yeah, "bon appétit" whatever you are inside Beezil.*

Mrs. Terrig seated Ann and me to the left side of the table. Two servants hovered around five men seated to the right. Although the men wore immaculately tailored suits, it was easy to picture them stalking children with night vision goggles.

The butler reappeared with a tray of crystal glasses and two decanters. He poured red wine into the glasses and extended the tray to Beezil. Beezil frowned then pointed at two of the glasses. The butler handed one to Ann, the other to me.

The wine tasted unusual. Probably expensive.

Everyone drank and chatted. While I didn't engage in the full width and breadth of the conversation, I agreed that the Terrigs' recent ailments were painful, their investments brilliant, the education system declining, and the lack of good stockbrokers baffling. During the conversation, Beezil seemed to be watching Ann and me with a compulsive interest, as if wondering how we could act like decent, solid citizens, and yet manage to keep straight faces. Raising his glass high, he proposed a toast.

"Here's to punk rock and all the bloody damage it's done to society."

I was polite. I said, "Absolutely," instead of "you're daft."

"I have to tell you that when I agreed to let you come here, I did so to please my wife—"

"—Nonsense," Mrs. Terrig said. It didn't seem like she'd meant to speak. It came out like an involuntary belch.

I made the appalling blunder of starting to laugh, then had to pretend I was choking. There seemed a general decision to let me choke, but Mrs. Terrig's maternal impulses got the better of her and she patted me on the back until I was breathing normally.

Beezil continued, "I wanted to kill you. You, the scum who sent my innocent, ingenuous daughter to her death. And yet, at the same time, I feel compelled to know what species of scum you are. Do you understand what I mean?"

"Absolutely," I said again.

"I wish I could explain my loss to you. But no words can explain it. So, what did you want to tell me?"

"You have my deepest sympathy. I do understand the untimely loss of family. But it's not too late to understand what your daughter believed in—believed was important enough to die for."

Ann handed Beezil a videotape.

"Kristin's face is electronically blocked out, but I think you'll recognize her by her clothes and body language."

Puzzled, Beezil took the videotape and turned it over several times.

"You document your own crimes?"

"We document illegal animal testing."

His tiny black eyes gleamed with enough hate to make me determined to stay in well lit, populated places. Before he could explode, I assuaged his hostility by telling him that Kristin was one of our finest, most trusted members. Dedicated, with a great talent for organization. The more I praised her, the more Beezil smiled. I needed him relaxed so I could catch him off guard when I told him that I had proof he'd hired someone to shoot Richard. It was a bluff. But I wanted to watch his reaction.

If I guessed right, he might freeze. He'd have a profusion of possibilities to analyze in a short time. Had someone witnessed the shooting? Had one of his staff been bribed? If I had evidence, how solid was it? Should he smile and bluff, or just throw us out? With all this swirling through his head, he might slip up and tell us something. As I talked and kept an eye on Beezil's five swanky thugs across the table from me, for the first time I realized a flaw in my strategy: if Beezil did slip up, he might want to shoot us a little.

With an occasional downward glance at my reflection in my wineglass to make sure I wasn't blurring with alcohol consumption, I kept up an enthusiastic stream of praise for Kristin. "She taught A.L.F. members, if arrested, not to be tricked by police into thinking another arrestee had already confessed. She taught them never to doubt the commitment of the others. Kristin had credibility and was a strong natural leader." I shifted my gaze from my glass to Beezil's eyes. "Your daughter would have been upset to know we have proof you hired someone to shoot Richard."

Mrs. Terrig pushed herself up out of her chair, knocking over her glass of wine.

"You're crazy!" She looked at me as though I were strolling through a shopping mall with a vacant stare and a chain saw.

Across from me, the five men in suits looked to Beezil for an attack command.

In Beezil's eyes was a lethal calmness. "If you have any evidence I had anything to do with any damned murder attempt, it's simply false. Sure, I had a motive: you robbed me of my only daughter. But hiring a hit man isn't exactly my style. I prefer a quieter, less messy approach—"

"—Poison?" I looked down woefully at the last two ounces of my drink. *It did taste peculiar, now that I think of it.*

"Hell no," his mouth twisted wryly. "More vicious than poison—"

The butler passed me a plate of crumb-size pieces of dessert. I passed it to Ann. They looked good, but I wanted to leave my mouth clear in case I had to talk, or in case I had to, for instance, beg for my life.

"—I'd hire lawyers. Lawyers who go for the throat, like the lawyer married to your ex-wife." A smile spread across his thin lips. "And lawyers with passion for their work, like Ms. Berlin."

I was impressed. Beezil had done his homework. Or, more likely, he'd had someone else do it and copied from their paper. However he'd gained knowledge of us, it deepened my concern about Bill sneaking onto a hunting trip with him.

"Lawyers," Beezil continued, "who ensure me that I'll be spending every penny you will ever make in your life, including social security. Lawyers who couldn't even start until I provided them with some evidence against you." He patted his breast pocket where he'd stored the A.L.F. tape.

"We'd like to negotiate," Ann said. I would have said it first, but the shock had made me swallow my tongue, and it took a moment to finish turning purple and suck a bit of air back into the old windpipe. "It's too late to return the dogs we took from your lab, but we'll promise to leave your lab alone—if you give us Brett Tarbatz's address, and if you promise never to reveal the names of any A.L.F. members."

"I can destroy you." Beezil spat out the words. "You damn well better return my dogs and you'd damn well better stay away from my buildings. I'll give you nothing—except a promise not to annihilate you until I *feel* like it."

Perhaps Beezil was entitled to his opinion of what constitutes generosity, but I felt he lacked certain qualities essential in a good host.

On Ann's face was a fiery, angry look unfamiliar to me: a hardened anger that aged her by ten years. She blurted out a word that I never even figured she knew.

"If you hurt the A.L.F., we'll go public with videos filmed in your lab before it burned. TV. Newspapers. Internet. The entire planet will see a daughter raid her daddy's test lab and know she died setting fire to it. It may mean nothing to you that Kristin died fighting against the work you do, work that supported her, but a lot of people will ask a lot of personal questions."

I expected an explosion from Beezil, but none came. He brought his hands together in front of him, clenched them together and squeezed. Then he pressed his lips against the knuckles of his thumbs.

"Okay. I'll forget what I know about the A.L.F. I'll even stop all animal testing in my lab, if you tell me who was responsible for my daughter's death? Who was with her? Who left her behind to die?"

"It's a deal," she said.

She's going to give away the driver?

"Wait," I said.

She didn't wait. "The fire wasn't part of the A.L.F.'s plan at all. Only one other person knew about it ahead of time, the same person who was supposed to get her out of there. Brett Tarbatz."

Beezil's face sagged like somebody had let the air out.

"That doesn't make sense. She was going out with Brett, he's heartbroken. . . ."

As Ann stood up, she said, "No one told her to start a fire."

Mrs. Terrig walked us to the front door. Ann put a hand on her arm.

"Please watch the tape. Call me if you have questions."

Mrs. Terrig smiled, but said nothing.

"Would you ask your husband to do one last favor for Kristin," I said. "Call off the attack on the organization that was closest to her heart."

Mrs. Terrig's expression gave perspective to the situation. It was like Forrest Gump looking at you saying, "You idiot. . . ."

"Good-bye," she said, "and be very careful."

* * *

I checked the rearview mirror. Ann tapped her fingers lightly on the dashboard.

We weren't being followed.

"What do we do now?" she asked.

"I think Ransacker will return to my room. Especially if we bait him."

"With what?"

"I was thinking I'd start a rumor at the Lobster tonight that the guy who shot Richard left behind a key that we're turning over to the police tomorrow."

"Did I miss something?" Ann asked. "What's the connection between the Ransacker and the Lobster?"

Through the windshield I watched the highway unfolding in our headlights.

"The timing just seems strange. Ransacker broke into my room while we were breaking into Richard's office. Maybe he knew somehow."

"You mean he sees us in the Lobster, then races to your

room?"

"Or calls someone else. Unless he's a psychic."

"Then why was he still there when you got back?"

"He couldn't have anticipated our getting caught and going home. And he wouldn't have left until he found whatever he was looking for."

"But why would he come back and search in the same place twice? Is it possible you believe this because you were recently clubbed over the head?"

I laughed hard and realized my ribs still ached.

"He may have shot Richard for something he thought Richard had with him, like the list of A.L.F. members."

"You're making some pretty fantastic leaps here."

"Maybe. But we know he was looking for something small because he poked into every cubbyhole. Small enough I might've had it with me when he broke in. So, if he knows we're away again tonight, he may return, hoping this time I left it home. If so, we'll catch him."

Ann pointed to the clearing sky. Stars were visible for the first time in days.

"I doubt this is going to work, Clark."

"Would it help if I told you that it did on an episode of *Columbo?*"

Ann rolled her lovely green eyes. I had a daring thought. I wondered how she would react if I put my arm around her.

* * *

I folded a flap from a Cracker Jack box and closed it between the door and jamb just below the bottom hinge. It would be nice to know if anyone went into my hotel room while I was gone.

Ann deposited Hoover on the back seat of the Dodge, got in, and opened the window enough for him to stick his nose out. I slid behind the wheel. At the Lobster, Hoover stayed in the car, wrapped in his blankets.

Petey greeted us at the door and shared a hug with Ann.

Over Ann's shoulder, Petey said, "It's tough, with Richard in the hospital and all."

I nodded. "Chas here tonight?"

Petey shook her head.

Mervyn had assumed command of the Lobster.

Wandering through the capacity crowd, mingling, groping about here and there, were three policemen pretending they weren't looking for Chas.

I ordered a diet soda and tried to look comfortable, as if I were staying a while. If Ransacker were present, I wanted him to think the coast was clear at my room. I was friendly and loud and did everything possible to draw attention to myself, short of tap dancing on a table.

A lot of people, many of whom looked suspicious, left during the first break. I found Ann and told her I'd pick her up at ten minutes before closing. On my way out I cornered Petey in front of the nativity scene.

"You remember that guy who climbed up on the stage the night Richard was shot?"

"That was Brett. He must've flipped out. He's been a quiet regular for years."

"What about the two guys who were egging him on?"

"Same friends he's always come in with. Chas might know them."

"Speaking of Chas, do you know why he went to jail?"

Petey's face stiffened. With anger, I think. "Six years ago he broke into a lab doing heart surgery on monkeys without anesthetics. He didn't know that one mad scientist was working late. The guy threw acid in Chas's face. That's how he got those awful scars. Plus a ten year sentence for breaking and entering."

***

I parked across from the Suite Night where I could see the window of my darkened room and half of the fire escape in the rear.

"It might be a long wait," I told Hoover, "but that's the

nature of sleuthing." He put his front paws on my thigh and wagged his tail, clearly impressed. Although I had told him several times I was sleuthing, I'd never actually explained what it was.

The skies darkened again and steady drizzle misted the buildings into a single gloom. Rain dripped off the car, gurgled in gutters, and splashed beneath the tires of passing cars. To help me stay awake I turned on the radio. The music stopped and a commercial told me about an industrial-strength bran cereal.

"I ate that stuff once," I told Hoover. "I don't mind being *regular*. But I was *unstoppable*." Hoover yawned. Apparently my revelation didn't alarm him.

Soon, I wanted to shut my eyes. *I'll just rest one eye at a time, so I won't fall asleep . . .*

Suddenly the car shook. I snapped my head up and reached into my pocket for the Luger replica. A cold gust of wind rocked the car again. I showed the Luger to Hoover, who sniffed it skeptically.

Sometime later I closed one eye again.

From out of the darkness a violent banging on the roof made me go cold with fear. Twisting, I saw a shadow peering intently at me from under the hood of a cape.

I fumbled with the door handle, trying to lock the door, but instead it popped open.

The shadow leaned inside. Hoover lunged forward, lapping at Ann's cheek.

I looked at my watch. "You left early."

"I was getting worried."

"How'd you get here?"

"Taxi." She held out her hand to help me climb out of the car. My legs wobbled, as though I had been asleep.

"You fell asleep."

"Nah."

"Very well. Then tell me, what time did the light in your room go on?"

I looked up. It *was* on. "I might've left it on."

"You turned it off. Now it's on. Somebody's been inside." We crossed the street.

"I'll bet I accidentally left it on."

"Bet? With what? What do you have, not counting your talking license-plate-holder?"

Let's see. I have a dryer-lint keepsake album. A wicker bowling ball. A Betty Rubble inflate-a-date. . . . I opened the door to the Suite Night. Ann asked the desk clerk if he'd seen any strangers pass. He yawned, and assured us he hadn't.

Ann swept past me with Hoover.

"I'll bet you a fancy dinner . . . wait. I've got a better idea. If I win, you tell me what *you* did that caused your marriage to end. What *you* take responsibility for."

"Why do you want to know that?"

"Because you'd rather gargle dirt than tell me."

Oh, please. I'd rather be dead in a ditch. "Okay. It's a bet. If I lose, I'll tell you about my divorce. If I win, you tell me something personal about your life."

"Like what?"

"Whatever I ask."

Ann started up the stairs.

"That's not fair."

"Exactly. Bet?"

"Bet."

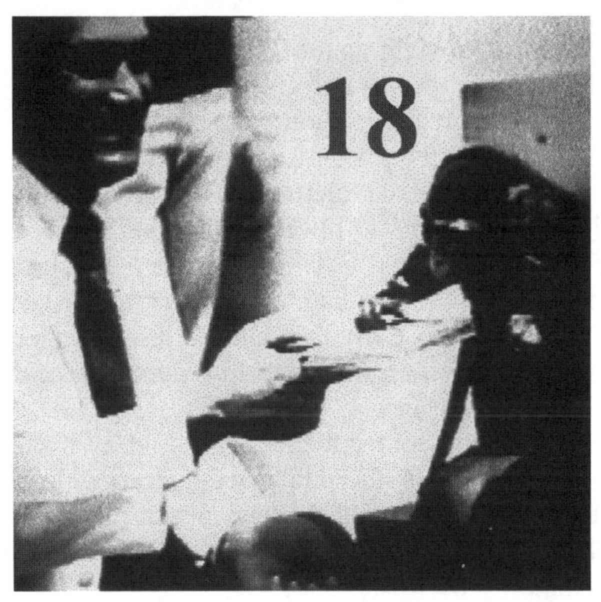

The folded Cracker Jack flap had that crumpled, stepped-on look I recognize from seeing myself in the mirror in the morning. Ann pulled me past the door and around a bend in the corridor.

I took the room key out of my pocket. Ann clenched my arm.

"Let's see who comes out."

Her plan, heavy on justice, was to wait and identify the culprit as he escaped. My plan, heavy on vengeance, was to catch him in the act and show him his large intestines.

"Wait here. If I'm not back in one minute, call the police."

We synchronized our watches like commandos, then I tiptoed down the corridor.

I pressed my ear to the door. Nothing. Standing off to the side, I slid the key gently into the lock, and turned it. Nothing. I opened the door a fraction, freeing the catch. I wiggled the key out and slipped it back into my pocket. Twisted the doorknob, tried to swallow, then shoved the door open and rolled back out of sight against the wall to the right of the door. Nothing jumped out at me.

But my couch and television were cockeyed to the wall. The short hairs at the nape of my neck stood like quills.

I crossed the threshold, alert as a deer. This time I looked behind the door. Nobody. I peered out onto the fire escape. Empty. Heart thumping, I stalked over to the bathroom.

Standing in front of the bathroom mirror, I watched as an odd expression crossed my face like I'd just taken a pitcher of ice water down my pants. *Why do I look so startled? Oh, yeah.* Ann won the bet.

At that moment, someone did a grand job of making me jump out of my skin by the simple act of clearing their throat behind me. In response, I flapped my arms, darted and ducked, bobbed and weaved—all while clearly expressing my dilemma to the world.

Help, however, had already arrived.

Ann flashed a big smile. "Did I scare you?"

"No. I periodically jump out of my skin for routine maintenance."

Hoover initiated an exhaustive snoofling check of the premises, bumping into furniture until I straightened it back to the way it had been. Ann sat on the bed. I went to the refrigerator and toyed with the door handle. I needed a drink badly, so I poured Canadian Club into two paper cups. Then I sat across from Ann, just squatted on the edge of the chair like I didn't want to use up too much of it. We drank in silence.

However, she kept grinning over her cup at me.

"Would it be possible for you to stop grinning?" I asked.

"I want details."

I stood and gazed out the window at the wet buildings glistening under the streetlights and began concocting diversionary tactics. Only when confident I could sidetrack her did I sit down again.

"I knew the *exact* moment our marriage was in trouble."

"Which was?"

"When I found my lunches packed in road maps with arrows pointing to Iraq."

"Bullshit," Ann said softly, but with feeling. Smoothly, she moved over to me and towered above my cowering figure. "Stop with the Howdy-Doody grin. You have less range of expression than the average fish. I'm not letting go of your collar until you tell me the truth."

"You don't have hold of—"

"I do now, Clark. A bet is a bet!"

"Let go of me!"

Grudgingly, she released my collar.

Slowly I began unruffling it.

"I'll help you get started," she said. "Bill told me that in every way that counted, you and Jessie were miles apart, with no road between you."

Oh no! If Ann knows part of the truth, how can I enhance it without risk?

"All right. I thought our marriage was perfect, until my wife said I was shutting her out." I knocked back the remainder of my drink and crushed the paper cup as though demonstrating an impressive feat of strength. Still thirsty, I began uncrumpling it. Ann waited quietly. Strangely, her silence was more encouraging than if she'd spoken.

"She said that I shared only the facts of my life with her, not the dreams." I held up the bottle of Canadian Club. Ann closed her eyes and shook her head. I poured myself another.

"After a while, I started to suspect Jessie was cheating on me. When I asked her about it, she told me about the forty-year-old divorce lawyer. I pleaded, 'Let's make our marriage work.' 'Make it work?' she said. 'You mean, give it a paper route or something?' The next day she was gone, leaving behind only a note."

"Saying?"

I stared at the ceiling, the cracks making rivers, the stains, lakes.

"'Each day is empty without shared feelings. You want forever, but I can't promise forever, empty in todays.' That's all she said. I thought there had to be more to it. I read the note over and over. Backwards and forwards. I think I even smelled it." I drained the last of my Canadian Club.

"We all make mistakes," Ann said. "We all have regrets. That's the price of being human. But eventually there's a point when guilt and remorse become self-indulgent. Examine the pain, then let it go."

There seemed magic in her observation. I felt something begin to unfurl inside me, like a plant uncurling its leaves and reaching toward the sun. Dredging up the past, examining the pain of my divorce, at long last I was breaking out of my self-imposed emotional isolation. Of course, I was drinking liquor straight out of the bottle at the time.

Emotionally spent, I yawned.

"What would you have asked me," she said, "if you had won the bet?"

"Tell me about the men in your life, starting with your dad."

"Both my parents died in a car crash when I was two. My grandparents raised me." She reached in her purse and pulled out two photos. In the first, a young couple holding a terrier smiled up at me from behind a judging table at a dog show. The pleasures of that day came through undiminished by the years. The second was a more recent photo of the same couple. They looked like duplicates of the first couple crumpled and smoothed out again.

Ann slipped the photos back into her purse and drew out two pieces of hard candy. She offered me one. I declined. Her eyes were sparkling.

"I've had one boyfriend."

I tried not to hyperventilate. "The guy in law school?"

"For three years."

"What happened?"

"We shared an apartment the third year. At first, everything was great. Then he decided I was suffocating him." The hard candy went from side to side in her mouth, like a die in a dice cup. Finally, she held it still. "At first he liked all my attention—then suddenly I'm a dry cleaning bag."

She can't be serious. "Any others?"

"A few, but compared to those, party streamers are permanent."

"Why?"

"You probably already know. Working with the A.L.F., other parts of my life vaporized. Most of my relationships were like passing ships—rocket ships—and ended with some heartfelt farewell like 'Lock up on your way out, would you, babe?'" She looked surprised, as if I'd been the one talking. "Listen to me prattle on. Anything else you'd like to know?"

Does every child who loses a parent build a wall around them? "Will you keep playing with Fluke, or go into law full time?"

"I'm staying with Fluke. That is, if Richard is okay. I mean, if Fluke continues. . . ."

"Wouldn't you make a lot more money as a lawyer?"

She nodded shyly.

"Are you bothered by their reputation?"

She grimaced in good humor. "Were I concerned about my reputation, I doubt I'd play in a rock band."

"The public does have a preconceived notion about the character of rock musicians."

"Especially female musicians. Men in the audience are convinced women are in a band only because they're sleeping with another band member. I think this belief dates back to the time when every 4-piece band included a corresponding number of girl tambourine players. And the women in the audience think you're a slut. If their boyfriend thinks you play well, then you're a cheap slut. I'm staying in Fluke because Fluke has become my family. Especially Corky."

"Are your grandparents gone?"

She nodded. "You know what? After they died it took years, but I learned to cope with loneliness. I really enjoy a quiet evening of reading. But the emptiness that comes over me when I think Fluke might break up is something new."

"Can I ask you something, Ann?"

"Uh-oh."

Does she know where I'm heading? I pressed on, aware I was on the precipice of asking her a question it might hurt her to answer. "This work you do, the child abuse cases . . ."

Her green eyes pierced the distance between us and she started nodding.

"If you don't want to talk about it right now, that's fine. But I'd like to hear about it when you're ready."

She swept her hair away from her eyes. "Thanks for understanding."

From fighting, my face was starting to bloat and soften like a melon going bad. I'd nearly lost a father figure. I was out of work and going to starve unless I learned some as-yet-undefined marketable skill. I understood nothing, but the concept of ignoring emotional problems until I could figure out ways to deal with the rapidly mounting backlog of concrete ones appealed to me.

Ann got to her feet. "Listen, I'll see you in the morning, okay?"

"And at night, at our 'family gathering' at Laurel." I stood, too.

She gave me a big warm hug. Having revealed so much of myself, I felt close to her.

"Want to stay here tonight?" After a moment of silence I added, "In case Ransacker returns."

"No, thank you." Her words showed she felt nothing of the closeness I was experiencing. Her tone was perfectly polite, her answer thoroughly reasonable, but all the same I felt it put distance between us, as if she'd taken several steps away.

"Lock your door, then," I said, hoping my voice betrayed

nothing of my unsettled thoughts.

She leaned forward, kissed my forehead, and fled without looking back. I walked into the kitchenette, alone. In single file. Intoxicated. Somehow I had reached excess without having ever passed through satisfaction.

Smuffkins ambled over and sat looking up at me. I watched her stretching her legs on the glass, reaching out, conveying, *Oh please pay attention to me. Please, love me.*

"Look at how much I loved Mom and Dad," I said. "Love ends in pain." I headed to the fridge for an Eskimo Whip. "I prefer what cholesterol does to the heart."

I watched rain washing down the window. I paced, drank Canadian Club, and wondered if I could face up to the foolish hope that Ann was my soul mate. I was ashamed of this fresh glimmer of hope, of the naiveté it revealed, the secret need, the quiet desperation.

I tossed the key left by the Ransacker into the top dresser drawer, then sat on the bed. Hoover, asleep on the floor, was dreaming, his legs twitched and he cried a little. For a long time I sat with my back against the wall. Eventually I fell asleep. Twice during the night I snapped the light on and tumbled out of bed to make sure the key hadn't disappeared. I listened to a man and a woman in another room threatening to have each other arrested, for what I had no idea, although I went into the hall twice hoping to find out.

I greeted the morning with a fairly spotty memory of the previous evening. One thing I remembered: stupidly asking Ann to stay the night. The bathroom mirror's reflected light struck the back of my skull, bursting inside. The prickly burrs of my hangover were mild compared to the sharp thorns of memory and self-awareness that bristled deeper inside my brain.

I called Ann and told her I was leaving to scout Laurel.

"You okay?" she asked.

"Didn't sleep much."

"Ever try counting sheep?"

"Never. Thinking about sheep while laying in bed is kind of weird to me."

Her laughter gave my headache a moment's relief, like rubbing a cramp.

***

To scout for the night's raid I drove north on Highway 1, then west on 128, away from Salem where not too many generations ago they burned witches. We entered a small farm town, Buffalo, with one industrial complex. Along the complex's east border was the Buffalo Bill Motel, a country bar called The Buffalo Stampede, a mobile-home park, and Laurel.

From the Buffalo Bill's roof I studied Laurel. Its test lab, an ordinary one-story brick building, was in a shallow canyon, its roof slightly above street level. The scientists, management, and maintenance crews were all local hires, which served the dual function of keeping labor costs low and security high. No one was going to do damage to the largest employer in the area, regardless of what they might see or hear.

I tested my walkie-talkie.

"Have any music?"

"No," a stolid voice said.

"How about sneakers, laced per code *one-two*?"

"Hold on, I'll put you through."

Corky answered and confirmed that everything was on schedule—vans painted, keys issued, updated codes and directions distributed.

I cracked a few marbles off the pavement below. A slingshot had replaced the Cobra, which had disappeared when the van crashed into the snow bank.

I drove the side streets and mapped everything. The Buffalo Stampede and the mobile home park presented a problem in that their entrances were only a block from Laurel, and The Stampede was open until three a.m. After my final surveillance pass, I headed home.

Back at the Suite Night I coated the pads of my fingers

with Elmer's glue and watched it dry nearly transparent, then pressed my fingers to the window to make sure the layer of glue was thick enough to cover the minute lines in my skin.

Ann came into my room wearing what appeared to be an evening gown that converted into a sleeping bag with a secret compartment for her head. All in black.

Then I made a terrible error.

I said, "I'm ready. Let's go."

Ann looked me over. "You're going to wear that?"

"Yes," I said hesitantly. "I think so."

"Nice outfit. Powder blue sports jersey, green pants, and a yellow shirt. You're dressed like the villain in a Batman movie."

"I don't understand." I studied her clothes. "Should I dress as if I'm going to an Amish funeral?"

"Do you consider yourself inconspicuous if you don't fluoresce when the lights go out?" She took me by the arm and led me to the bathroom mirror. I leapt out of it. Behind me, she blended in with the shadows.

She went to my closet and pulled out layers of drab.

"But those are my *good* clothes."

"Should be easy to replace them. The Salvation Army has a really nice selection in your basic taste."

19

Ann and I started down the alley of the industrial complex. Small factories lined both sides, and shadows were everywhere and deep. After one block, I had the briefest sensation of movement near me. My breath stopped on the half exhale. I glanced over my shoulder and saw . . . nothing.

"What?"

"Nothing. I thought I saw a shadow move."

As we walked I looked for stirring in the Dumpsters, motion behind dismantled cars, faces in windows. Each time we put the light from a factory behind us, I watched our shadows in front of us. In the corner of my eye, there was a shadow where there shouldn't have been a shadow. When I turned my head, it was gone.

Then I heard something. Close.

Ann saw it first. I followed her gaze upward.

A bird swooped across the hazy moon, paused, dropped something shiny, and soared away. No. It wasn't a bird . . . but a giant black wasp. No. It can't be. It is. The missing Cobra.

Ann gasped and fell to the ground. In the moonlight I

saw a dart stuck in her upper thigh.

I wrapped my arms around her waist and pulled her back into the shelter of the nearest doorway. She was trembling, but made no sound as I eased the dart out. Razor-sharp, it had penetrated an inch into her leg. The feel of her warm blood on my hand made me shake with rage as much as with fear.

We stayed in the shadows, unable to tell whether we could be seen. I forced myself to breathe silently when I wanted to pant like a dog. Watching the sky, I saw only clouds streaming across the moon.

The Cobra swept suddenly up over the rooftops, glided back down, and hovered. Its bay doors opened. A glint of light flashed. I dodged, but a dart punctured my jacket and skinned my arm.

I looked for motion and listened for footsteps. Over the monologue of the blustery wind I heard cars sloshing down streets and country music twanging from The Buffalo Stampede.

The hovering sound came again without warning.

A dart hit the trashcan next to me. I may have broken all national long jump records, but I'll never know, because while the can was still rattling, I carelessly rolled away from the icy spot where I'd landed without stopping to mark it.

"After the next pass," I whispered, "let's make a run for it." I handed Ann a trashcan lid to hold over her head.

We were crouched, leaning back slightly to get power for a quick start, when a pistol crack echoed among the buildings and sent pigeons hurtling upward from their rooftop perches.

"He's trying to pin us down while the helicopter circles," I said.

"Why not just shoot us?"

I braced my back against the wall, searching for our ambusher in the all-consuming blackness, then I twisted off my right shoe. Ann turned her head this way and that, glaring at me as if one eye had seen what the other had reason to doubt.

"Don't worry," I said. "I've seen Maxwell Smart do this."

"This is hardly the time for humor," Ann said, although I wouldn't have had much trouble deducing that from her tone of voice.

On the Cobra's next pass I heaved the shoe with all my strength. I watched the shoe sail upward toward its target . . . until gravity noticed it.

As it fell harmlessly into a Dumpster, a dart ripped my left ear and blood spit over me. I lost my footing in the slush and landed hard on the cold pavement. Trying to get up too fast, I flopped around like some pathetic salmon whose central nervous system had been destroyed by toxic waste. I took in a lungful of the damp night air, and got to my feet.

"You all right?" Her eyes were liquid with concern.

I put my hand to my burning ear and pulled it away soaked with blood. It felt as if tongs had been jammed into my brain. *Shit, it hurts!* The pain overloaded my senses and somehow crystallized them. Instead of confusion and fog, everything seemed clearer.

I yanked off my other shoe and pulled the laces out of all but the bottom two holes. Holding a trashcan lid over my head, I started across the alley pulling Ann behind me. As the Cobra banked in front of us, I dropped the lid and whipped the shoe high and hard, end over end. The shoe missed, but a lace caught in the Cobra's blades, which caused it to dip and wobble. Controlling it would be a two-handed job now.

The ambusher overcorrected and the bird spun, becoming a small black electric fan. A down draft caught it and dashed it against a building. Ann and I ran across the alley. Footsteps echoed away above us.

We hobbled into the delivery entrance of the motel, our cheeks red with cold and panic, our clothes bloodstained and torn, but we felt safe. Marginally.

* * *

"You would've been better off," Ann said, "if you hadn't looked in a mirror for a couple of days." We were squeezed into the bathroom. Blood was smeared over my cheek. I clutched my stinging left ear with the vague idea of holding it on.

Ann pressed both hands over her eyes as if they burned, then turned on the tap. Brown water oozed, seeming full of the sort of things you might find wriggling around in a glass of the Ganges River. I washed, then found a stiff towel and flapped my hands with it a couple of times.

Ann's wound was worse than mine, deeper. It was a tribute to her strength she didn't complain of the pain. But it also kept me from complaining like I really wanted to. Instead I moaned quietly to myself.

It was ten minutes to the start of the Laurel mission.

Ann leaned against me. "That man on the roof was waiting for us."

"He didn't seem to be trying very hard to kill us, only to delay us. Ann! You're turning a color I don't even recognize."

"That probably means he knows the *timing* of our plans. We'd better call off the mission. Give me the walkie-talkie."

I pulled it out. The back was open, the antenna broke, and the batteries gone. "Must've happened when I jumped and rolled."

Ann grabbed the phone and dialed.

"No answer. They're on their way."

"Right into a trap."

"Let's get over there," she said.

Am I willing to walk into a trap to save rabbits? To save the A.L.F.? To get revenge for Richard? To please Ann?

"Clark?" Ann's voice broke in on my thoughts. "Clark, are you listening to me?"

I blinked. Ann wanted an answer to some question I hadn't heard her ask.

"Are you there, Clark?"

"Yes."

"What were you thinking?"

"Nothing."

"You aren't telling the truth."

"I know it."

"Are you having second thoughts?"

I paused. "Tonight is big, isn't it?"

"Yes. Remember it's more than just Laurel. Other cosmetic companies use government grants as a source of income. We're sending a message to them not to rely on grants and bogus research for profit."

"If anyone knows we're coming, they'll be a more immediate threat to us than the police. Instead of scouting from this roof, it'll be better if you come with me. If the lab is heavily guarded, you'll be in position to keep the A.L.F. from walking into a trap."

Ann sighed and rested her head on my shoulder. It filled me with a sense of completeness. Her arms slipped around me, and nothing had ever felt better—her hair against my cheek, her hands on my back, her warmth, her lilac scent.

It was hard to believe I'd known her less than a year.

"Let's go."

The wind had stopped and an eerie calm hung in the air. A sign posted at the edge of the Laurel compound read PRIVATE PROPERTY—NO TRESPASSING. It was a large sign, and it shielded our approach as we clambered over a four-foot-high snow bank, then ran across the parking lot to the darkest corner of the test lab.

I pressed my ear to each door and window before checking to see if it was locked. They all were. At one window I heard the faint sound of a TV but couldn't see anything.

On the far side of the lab, I whispered to Ann, "It sounds as if the guard is watching TV. If I can pry open a window or a door, I can throw him a surprise party."

I stuck a piece of a guitar string into a door lock and twisted and pried. It was a heavy lock, and a good one. I moved to a window. Suddenly, a bright light flashed on me from behind. I squatted low. Just a passing car. But it meant I could be seen from the road.

I worked quickly on the window, occasionally glancing around, doing a very bad impression of a guy minding his own business. I forced the outer corner of the window away from the frame to get a grip on it with my fingertips. Pulling the corner, I slid a guitar pick along the top toward the hinged edge, making the opening steadily wider until a sudden click-clack sound came from the bottom of the window as the ratchet slipped two notches. I pulled harder and the ratchet gave way with a sound slightly louder than the clap of Creation.

I wanted to run. Instead, I slipped my hand inside and opened the window.

"If the guard grabs me, call the police while you're running."

"Running?"

"Like a cheap pair of stockings."

She squeezed my hand. I snaked in through the window.

The room gave off a cloying odor, the sickly-sweet commingling of chemicals and dead flesh. I could only imagine what lay in front of me as I waited for my eyes to adjust.

Slowly the gigantic laboratory came into dark focus. Glass-fronted cabinets lined the wall to my left. Electrical cords crisscrossed the floor. Down the center ran stainless steel tables on which a half-dozen dead rabbits were displayed in varying stages of dissection. Along a wall were workbenches with rows of rabbit stockades used for Draize testing.

One runty white rabbit was still headlocked, squirming in listless denial. I put a hand over my flashlight and turned it on for a moment. The rabbit looked back at me with cloudy, blistered corneas that could barely see, yet I sensed were hopeful.

I'll come back for him.

I stuck my hand in my pocket, found the pistol's handle, and accidentally squeezed the trigger. Fortunately it wasn't loaded, so I didn't spritz myself. I raised the pistol up next to my head and listened. I placed one foot in the hallway, heard a voice, and snapped my foot back.

Chicken! I was angry with myself. I wanted to be angry.

Not that this was a particularly good time for self-appraisal. Anger held back the fear. The two emotions danced together divinely, anger leading a swirling performance at the core of my being.

So much for being able to think.

As I moved down the hallway toward a thin strip of light flickering under a door, I wondered if my approach to life had been too simplistic: *Be happy, try not to hurt anyone, and hope I fall in love.* I wanted to know if Ann could ever love me. I wanted to know if the Laurel guard was waiting behind the door with an ice pick dipped in rat poison. There was a lot I wanted to know before I died.

I inhaled, shoved the door open, threw myself forward into a fast roll, banged my head against the leg of a table, heard something shatter, then sprang to my feet with the water pistol square on the guard's stunned expression.

Assuming a shooter's stance, I gripped the gun with both hands as if it would kick.

"Freeze!"

Although the guard didn't move, I kept the gun on him. A smell like food gone bad made me slightly dizzy. Leaning against the wall, I tried to look alert while I let my head clear.

The guard was mostly in shadows, leaning back in a large executive chair, light from a portable television washing over him in the violent colors of a modern Technicolor bloodbath. His expression mildly vampirish, as if the joke were on me.

I groped the wall for the light switch and flipped it on. Bathed in green fluorescent light, everything looked so sharply different that I might have been changed into another kind of creature with differently made eyes. My world had suddenly changed.

The guard was Lester Gillis. I sagged back against the wall. It was as if I'd just scored a touchdown, spiked the football to the ground, and it bounced up and smacked into my knicky-knacks.

His neck was topped with a bloody pulp that had once been a face. Even his eyes weren't where they were supposed to be, and seemed to be peeping at me from around a side of hanging beef. Nausea gripped my insides.

I unlocked the front door and whispered, "Ann?"

She came churning through the doorway so fast that she saw Lester's body before I could block her view. She clapped both hands to her cheeks, then over her mouth.

I approached the body, slipped on the bloody floor, and grabbed the arm of the chair to keep from falling. A can of Body Slam Malt Liquor dropped onto the floor and rolled five feet until it stopped against a bloody bible.

I poked around on Lester's neck. No pulse, but he was still warm—his killer couldn't be far away. To better hear, I turned off the TV.

"Now what?" Ann whispered. "If we free the rabbits, the A.L.F. gets blamed for the murder."

Outside, a van rolled to a stop, lights out. I opened the door to the lab. Corky came in first. Behind her, a man in a fake wig and mustache was pushing a laundry cart.

"We should abort," I said. "Something's wrong. It may be a trap."

"We're already here. If it's a trap, we're in it. If it isn't a trap, let's do our job." She followed Wig down the hall, opening doors.

"Empty."

Wig, his voice familiar, said "Empty," from the next room. Corky raced to the next door. "Empty."

"Nothing here either." Wig was Mervyn.

Had the experiment ended? Had the rabbits been killed?

"Here!" Corky cried. "Rabbits!"

Ann gripped my shoulder. She said something, but I wasn't listening carefully until her nails penetrated.

"The test procedures."

We headed the other way down the corridor. At an

intersection she nudged me to the left and took the right.

The dark hall stretched in front of me. My heart thumped. The first door was metal with a small rectangular window just below eye level. I peered in, but the lights were out, so I cracked the door open. Standing outside, I reached inside with my left hand, fumbling for the light switch. I expected something to charge out at me—or to put its hand over mine as I patted the wall in search of the switch plate.

Nothing did.

I found the switch. Lights illuminated bloody surgical pliers and a hacksaw with pieces of bone and rabbit fur in its teeth. Mesh cages, empty, lined three walls. Tentatively, I stepped inside, leaving the door open.

Two file cabinets stood against the far wall. The first was labeled "Test Procedures." *Eureka*! Foregoing caution, I crossed the room and pulled drawers. They flew open, empty.

The second cabinet, marked "Technical Papers," held hundreds of articles already published in medical journals. In the rear of the bottom drawer was a file containing three research papers stamped "confidential." I stuffed them into my jacket pocket.

Back in the hallway a laundry cart nearly ran me down. Without losing momentum, Mervyn waved an apology. I checked the other rooms along the hall, but none had the procedures.

I met Ann at the intersection where we'd parted. We searched each other's eyes for signs the other had found the illegal procedures. I saw the change in her face, the swift darkening of her eyes, and knew it was mirrored in my own.

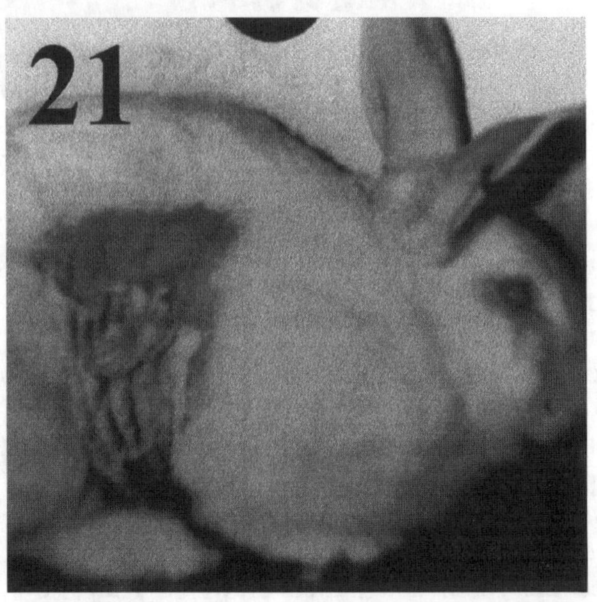

21

Ann's arms were across her stomach, holding herself like something broken. I put my arms around her and held her close. She pushed me away and looked into my eyes.

"Maybe they hid the procedures in a safe somewhere."

"Why would they? They didn't expect anyone to steal those . . . okay, our plans may have been leaked. Let's look."

I followed her into an office labeled "Jonathan Laurel, President." She went straight to an interior French door and pulled on it. It bowed, but didn't open. I gripped the handle and yanked. The door flew open, I lost my balance and fell backward. The dim ringing in my head was shrouded by a burglar alarm shrieking like a wounded banshee.

We ran out of the office.

"I have to get one last rabbit," I said. "Start the van."

"No! We have to leave *now*."

I dashed back to the testing area and took a wrong turn.

Where am I? To hell with it—I found a bank of light switches and flipped them all on.

Strange how light changed the size and complexity of the

lab. Now it was smaller and more simply arranged. I found the stockade room, freed the small white rabbit and grasped him by the neck. As I ran through the front door I heard a police siren blare. Then a gunshot. No. Thunder.

Needles of rain stung my sliced ear as I climbed the slope. As I reached the van, a police cruiser squealed around the corner. Ann pushed the door open. I jumped in, holding the rabbit to my chest. I closed the door as quietly as I could but it sounded as if someone had dropped one steel slab on top of another.

The cruiser screeched to a stop behind us. We locked our doors and slid to the floor. I held the squirming rabbit tightly under me. Our only prayer was the police being drawn to the alarm.

Car doors opened. Lifetimes passed. A flashlight played over the dashboard, then the driver's seat. Someone tried to open the door. I squeezed my eyes shut.

Suddenly, a bloodcurdling scream: "Help! Rape!" Corky's agonized voice.

Two pairs of heavy footsteps ran toward the scream. I lifted my head. In the side mirror I saw people pouring out of The Buffalo Stampede and the mobile home park.

After ten seconds, Ann started the engine and we raced away. Time began to behave normally again.

Neither of us spoke until Ann said it wasn't such a good idea for me to go back for one more rabbit, that I was stubborn and a schmuck and a moron and a copious amount of other unflattering things. I listened to it all patiently and, when she was finished, I held up the tiny white rabbit and said, "How could I leave Alice?" at which point Ann proceeded to run down the whole list of my attributes again, even finding new ones.

"That bible by Lester's body," I said. "Bill?"

"What, he killed Lester in a struggle?"

"Hopefully, in self-defense."

"Lester was sitting in a chair."

"Maybe Bill made some deal for the procedures, then left."

"Why was Lester guarding Laurel?" Ann asked. "And who would go there to kill him?"

"He threatened Chas."

"I should have grilled Chas about that blackmail message. And kept my plan to talk with Lester."

"Lester would've seen an opportunity to blackmail the A.L.F. And everything that happened still would have happened." I was overstating my point. I wasn't sure that I had a point, and I was overstating it.

"Somehow," she said, "*my* priorities got jumbled up." I had never heard Ann use sarcasm, but what she did with the word "my" was a wonder to behold.

"Our agendas were different from the start," I said. "Mine included revenge. I'm pretty sure I told you that. So don't act surprised. . . ."

"Well, I . . ." She took her eyes off the road, far too long, and glared at me as though I had said, "Think I'll get an axe, since it's a stormy night, and do away with you."

We lapsed into silence. I became aware of the rain turning into sleet. After several miles, Ann reached to turn on the radio. I gently touched her wrist. She batted my hand away.

WOPPITTY WOPPITTY WOPPITTY! A horrible sound emanated from beneath us. Ann directed the van onto the shoulder and slid to a stop.

"I'll change the tire." Before Ann could respond I handed Alice to her, then stepped out into the freezing rain.

After fifteen cold, wet, miserable minutes, I managed to get the tire changed. I put my nose to Ann's window and when she rolled it down I wiped the rain off my face and tried, "Sorry."

"Sure." People make mistakes, her tone implied. But I sensed things were not exactly wonderful between us.

"Want me to drive?"

She slid over. When I climbed in, she was still sulking, but watching me get soaked seemed to have mellowed her a little. She opened the glove box, rummaged through some tapes, and made a thoughtful selection. She popped a B-52s tape in the player and turned up the volume so she couldn't hear me if I decided to talk.

I took the first exit and headed south on gloomy, unlit back roads. She navigated us onto a narrow lane that dead-ended at a dance hall. FRAT PARTY proclaimed a sign above the door, and music blared from inside. I parked.

The same bulldog face that had guarded the U-Rent shed was now guarding the dance hall entrance.

"In their behavior toward creatures," Ann said to the guard, "all men are Nazis." He stepped aside to let us in.

Corky, Dr. Dean, and a couple dozen operatives in disguise were examining rabbits in cages. Six operatives ran outside to unload the rest of them from our van.

An unnatural silence fell over the room as word spread we hadn't recovered the test procedures. The mood improved slightly with the news that most of the rabbits needed only minor medical treatment.

Alice was the only seriously injured survivor. Visible shimmers shook her flanks as I carried her to the table. Dr. Dean gave her two shots and put some drops in her eyes.

"She'll be okay."

"In two days we'll take her to the Peace Plantation with the others," Corky said.

Ann turned the music down.

"Wonderful job, everyone. We saved five-hundred rabbits tonight."

"Our next mission," Corky said, "in three weeks, is the rescue of ten chimpanzees scheduled to be shot in the head by bastards—pardon me, researchers. Not to study head injuries, but to test the effectiveness of the bullets."

* * *

While I drove to the Suite Night, Ann was quiet. Something was on her mind. I kept up a line of polite chatter and waited her out.

Finally she asked, "Did you mean what you said about Bill leaving that bible? Couldn't it have belonged to Lester?"

"Maybe. But I recognize Bill's taste in bibles. In fact, I have a nice collection of them myself. I'll call him when we get back."

"Things got out of control. Someone broke rank. That 'rape' scream was an old recording and not part of tonight's decoy plan. Who could've done that?"

An intriguing question, but I was unable to come up with an answer by the time we reached the Suite Night. Hoover greeted us enthusiastically. He was always glad when I returned, as if astounded any creature with such an inferior sense of smell could find its way home.

Ann put Alice on the floor. Alice's flanks shivered as she tried to make herself into a tiny, invisible rabbit. Hoover approached, sniffing cautiously. When his nose was an inch from her, he froze. I wondered if he had any idea what a rabbit looked like. I was sure he knew the smell of fear.

He gently licked Alice's face. She twitched her nose, then relaxed. Hoover lay down while Alice hopped around, exploring the room. Then she came back and snuggled up against Hoover. His tail thumped once.

I called home and reached our answering machine.

"Bill, please call me." I hoped it wasn't too late for him to hear the message. "I love you."

Ann smiled one of the prettiest smiles I'd ever seen. But it didn't last long.

"It seems someone knew we were coming, but didn't call the police. They killed Lester and took the test procedures. Who would hate the A.L.F. enough to set us up by killing someone?"

"I wonder if the police are after us now?"

"If not now, soon. They've already found Lester, and they want to blame Fluke if they can—with the missing rabbits, that leads them to the A.L.F."

"Any other way to tie the A.L.F. to this?"

"Two ways. Brett may still be a loose cannon. And certainly the Laurel employee who tipped us off, when he hears there was a murder, will admit that he gave us a key. We promised him we wouldn't hurt anything."

"Maybe the police will wait to interrogate the employees when they return to work Monday."

"If we don't find the killer before then, the A.L.F.'s future is bleak." Ann's eyes were lifeless, emptied of their spark.

"Let's get some sleep," I said. "In the morning we'll terrorize vast portions of Cavalry until someone confesses to Lester's murder. Then we'll do lunch."

Ann stood, straightened her shoulders and with an exhausted sigh said good-night. After several pounding heartbeats, she went to her room.

Four hours later, drenched with icy sweat and trembling, I came bounding awake from a nightmare so terrifying I couldn't remember any part of it. I fell back asleep wondering what seeped through my subconscious and so thoroughly chilled my blood.

By the time the pink-orange parfait of dawn touched the rooftops, I'd woken up in a reasonably good mood, the nightmare nearly forgotten. Even the self-portrait of the dairy cow looked pleasant. Instead of getting up, I lay in a half-doze. Faint images percolated to the surface of my brain. They came faster and stronger, rushing toward me like subway stations seen from the front of a speeding train, melting and flowing into one another as they do in a dream.

One image kept recurring. A bleeding bible.

I got dressed, fed Alice and Hoover, and dropped a slice of wheat bread in the toaster. Then I called my sister.

"Have you ever doubted Bill's loyalty to the A.L.F.?"

"What do you mean?"

"Animal-rights philosophy conflicts with his religious

beliefs. Maybe he's found allies and turned against us."

"Are you crazy?"

"Let me explain—"

"Can you do it without using the words 'alien abduction'?"

"That hinders me, but I'll try anyway." The toaster billowed smoke. I stretched the phone cord to the toaster and forced the toast out. "How many people can fly the Cobra that attacked Ann and me?"

"Holy cow, do you know what you're saying? He's our brother!"

I began scraping charcoal off the toast. "Our dear brother helped Brett onstage. They use the same religious rhetoric. Just before Richard was shot, Bill sent me outside while he stayed inside. At the hospital, he kept asking me *not* to go hunt for the gunman—"

"Nobody wanted you to hunt for the gunman. Your newly acquired suspicious nature makes you a good detective, but a deeply troubled person. Can you really imagine Bill purposely hurting anyone?"

I looked at the toast in my hand. Corky was right. It was easier to imagine what it would be like to drink from a gutter, or dig toast out of a trashcan and eat it.

* * *

A distant radio played early Rolling Stones, muffled and distorted, as if Mick Jagger were singing "Ruby Tuesday" with a sock stuffed in his mouth. In a long green skirt, Ann stood with her back to the window, she with her thoughts, me with a bottle of Diet Cola. Despite the glum look on her face, her presence lit up the room. Buried in our silence was the tension from the previous day.

Eventually she said, "Did you say something?"

"Don't think so. Rainy morning."

"Yes. Rainy."

Hoover paced between us, trying to get our attention, insecure in the changed mood. I picked at the label from my Cola bottle, an unpleasant habit which I had, up until that

40

moment, never stooped to.

"You mad at me?"

Casting equal glances between me and through the frosted windowpane, she seemed to make up her mind.

"Just the world."

"Well, all right. That I can understand."

She picked up the phone and dialed.

"Mrs. Terrig please. This is Ann Berlin . . . Hello Mrs. Terrig. Did you get a chance to watch that tape?" She mainly listened for the next few minutes, said good-bye, and hung up.

"The Terrigs watched the tape. They recognized Kristin. They were surprised she was such an ardent leader. For the first time since her death they went into her bedroom where they found A.L.F. literature and Kristin's notes. They came to understand she thought of all animals the way they think of their poodle, Mitzi. The literature reminded them of conversations they'd had with Kristin about animal testing. Conversations they hadn't taken seriously. She said thank you."

Ann headed for the door. Hoover chugged after her and jumped at his leash. She patted him.

"Be back soon."

I almost bounced my theory off her that Bill was involved. But Jim Rockford once said, "Don't let speculation water down proven truths. Leap to conclusions when that is the only way to safety." I needed more information before I was ready to tie the laces on my ballet shoes, slip on my tutu, and leap to any conclusion that tied Bill to a murder.

I settled in front of *Barnaby Jones* with Hoover and Alice.

What's the first sign of insanity? Had Bill met the requirements when he began collecting bibles? When he started giving them away to people who "need a good talking-to from the Lord?" Or will it be when he starts autographing them?

I enjoy watching detective shows, but I'm not good at

figuring them out. What it takes for me to crack a case is for someone to tell me who did it. Not today. When *Barnaby* ended, I still hadn't closed the case, but something was in the back of my mind. The only way to draw it out was to make my mind go blank.

I gazed through the rain at rusty fire escapes. My mind wandered. I tried to remember how to reset my digital watch. A blank.

Bingo. My mood was suddenly buoyant.

Nobody had broken into Laurel to kill Lester—all the entrances had been locked. Lester must have opened the door for his killer. And Bill wouldn't have knocked politely and asked to be let in.

It might help the police solve the murder if I told them what I knew—but they would ask *how* I knew, and the answer would tie me to the murder site.

A jolt of fear shot through me. I didn't want to go to jail and leave Ann and Hoover. I looked at Hoover. "You don't worry about tomorrow, do you?"

As if in answer, he chuffed and gave me a look that said he doubted that I knew what dogs worried about.

"If I'm arrested, Corky will care for you as well as I have."

He cleared his throat as if he really hated to point out that the canned food I gave him wasn't likely to be a featured item on the dessert cart in canine heaven.

I put a bowl of food down. Alice hopped right over. Then she looked back at Hoover, waited, then thumped her hind foot. Hoover came over. Alice didn't start eating until Hoover did.

I spent the next five minutes with my fingers hovering over the telephone, almost deciding to call the police. Finally I dialed.

"Chief Patti York speaking."

"I'm calling with some information about the shooting of Richard Tipton."

She drew in a dramatic deep breath as if mine were the tenth call today giving her leads.

"You sound like a concerned citizen. Thank you. Don't worry, we're doing everything we can."

"I was attacked from a roof, perhaps by the same guy. I can give you a dart he may have left fingerprints on."

"Okay," she said as thrilled as if I had promised to brush my teeth after every meal. "You need to come to the station and file a report."

"I see. Where's the station?"

"1775 Ironside Avenue. Near the Vinyl Fetish."

"Be right there." After I hung up, it occurred to me the Chief had insinuated something about my character when she used the Vinyl Fetish as a landmark.

I took a paper bag, poked two eye holes in it, folded it, and slipped it into my jacket pocket with the belief I had a constitutional right to hide my face, at least until the police obtained a search warrant. Then I decided to leave the bag home. It's the simple type mistake that can lead to years of unsettling conversations with prison psychologists.

Departing, I told Hoover that he was in charge of everything. This didn't appease him. He flattened his ears against his head and put one paw in my hand. "See you soon," I said, turning off the light. As I began closing the door, he stuck his snout in the narrowing crack. He sniffed at me and tried to lick my hand. I was afraid I was going to pinch his nose, but he stepped back at the last moment.

I hailed a taxi. The yellow cab swerved to the curb, hit the brakes, and was moving again as I pulled the door closed. Staying low in my seat, I told the cabby to rush to the Vinyl Fetish and keep an eye out for anyone following us. He nodded okay in the rearview mirror, but his expression changed. He seemed generally wary of me and leaned forward in his seat a little, as though I might suddenly bite him or something.

He dropped me off without pulling over to the curb. I

paid him, although not until I got the pleasure of seeing his face when I said, "Pay? I was hitchhiking."

Standing two doors from the police station, I canvassed its entrance out of the corner of my eye and whistled like you do in a graveyard at night to chase away the willies.

As I shuffled sideways in front of the Vinyl Fetish, I looked up at the glossy face of a plastic mannequin. She wore tight vinyl clothes and held her arms and hands in a position that looked as if somebody had just snatched her guitar away and she hadn't had time to react.

I sidled past her and stood in front of the drugstore between the Fetish and the police station. Before I could work up nerve enough to go inside, its door opened and out stepped the same huge, boneless officer who had questioned me in the hospital. He was talking with someone, who, from the thickness of his glasses and the drone of his speech, I guessed had more than a nodding acquaintance with computers.

I can't loiter here. I'll pretend I'm window-shopping. Browse in this drugstore window for a moment and—oh, my, the only window at hand and it has to be devoted entirely to feminine napkins!

Heat stealing into my face, I crept behind the officers and into the station.

The receptionist at the front desk ignored me. Dressed in a crushed velvet suit, she reminded me of an Oriental doll. She was filing her fingernails on an emery board with such intense concentration that a casual onlooker might suspect it was the most important thing she had to do for the rest of her entire day.

I drifted past her into an office labeled "Police Chief Patti York." It was empty. I rapped my knuckles firmly on the desk. From an adjacent room a female voice with authority said, "Just a second."

Strewn over the Chief's desk were printed forms and mugshots. An African violet bloomed next to a CB radio and a photograph of what probably was her husband and teenage daughter. A few seconds later she came out and sat behind the desk. A big, muscular woman, she wore eye makeup, tomato-red lipstick, and probably more subtle stuff I didn't know about.

My fear of going to jail returned.

She beckoned me to sit down with a slow wave, then motioned me to pass her a ceramic cigarette case containing a pack of Virginia Slims just out of her reach. I handed her the ceramic case which she took gingerly, with just her thumb and index finger, as though she misunderstood the warning on the cigarette's package.

Leaning back, she looked at me with all the detachment of a child of the '90s watching a teacher. She knew I was there, but didn't know exactly why.

"Who are you?"

"I'm, uh, Barney Rubble."

"Look, Barn . . . Ah, you damn wise guy." Her face reddened. "You're not Barney. That was Fred's neighbor."

"Caught me."

"Why are you here?"

"Well . . . er . . . a friend told me to tell you about the person who shot Richard." *A friend, yeah, that's it.* "The gunman has . . . um . . . broken into my friend's hotel room and shot at him from a rooftop. I'm here to give you information that might help you catch the gunman before anyone else in your town gets shot."

She pressed her hands together, brought them to her mouth, and blew some air between them.

"What's the capital of Massachusetts?"

"Massachusetts?"

"Right."

Is this a trick question? "It's Boston."

"Correct. Did you know your face changes when you tell the truth?"

I cast my two faces downward.

"Now—who are you?"

"The guy who just called."

I handed her one of the darts. She took it by the steel feathers, looked it over, then placed it on the ceramic cigarette case.

"I'll check it for prints." She leaned her elbow on the desk and pointed her lit cigarette at me. "Maybe you should tell me what you know."

She listened with a worried frown as I told her about the night Richard was shot and about somebody ransacking my room. I could see her figuring out more than just what I was telling her.

When I finished, she said, "Are you one of those animal-rights activists?" much as another person might have said, "There's vomit on this seat."

I began to nod, but twisted the nod into a neck stretch.

"I'm familiar with their cause. . . ."

"Well, are you familiar with anyone who recently burned down the Terrig Laboratory? It's just us here. You can talk freely."

I kept freely silent. She had already figured out too much.

She asked me what I knew about Lester's murder. She discussed it with me quite thoroughly and, I thought, with some suspicion. The difference between our discussion and an interrogation was not bigger than a bread box. She concluded by telling me not to leave town. That was a switch. A cop telling me not to leave town.

I became annoyed.

"Are you going to help me?"

She gave a big sigh, like I was asking for an organ donation.

"Let's suppose, for the sake of your argument, this gunman has an *unreasonable* motive to target you. What can I do? Teach you karate?"

I leaned forward, rudely putting my elbows on her desk. I meant to be rude.

"Are you planning to just sit around and wait for the gunman to come waltzing in and confess?"

"Not a bad idea, actually." She leaned over her desk, shoving junk from one side to the other. *Probably considers that a good day's work.* "When someone shoots an animal-rights activist, you'd think they'd step forward and take credit for it, wouldn't you?"

I sat back. "What do you think animal-rights activists are? Lunatics?"

"I have no proof if that's what you mean." She smashed both fists on her desk where my elbows had been. Pencils in a plastic cylinder jumped. "Due to activists like you, Mr. Terrig demands extra police protection. It places an additional burden on my already overburdened staff."

"Mr. Terrig can afford to hire his own security."

"He doesn't have to. As the major employer here, he has political clout. I'm an elected official. Thanks to you, when Terrig rebuilds his plant, he'll probably make me guard it myself. Do you know what I'd like better than anything else in this world?"

My head on a stick? "No."

"I'd like to watch subversives like you die. Slowly. For a month maybe. Maybe longer. If I ever catch one, I'll personally see to it he shares a jail cell with an eyeball collector."

An eyeball collector? Ha. Chief York. Some kidder.

Kidding aside, I felt lousy. My opinion of myself at any given moment is heavily dependent upon the last thing I've heard said about me, whether said by a dear friend or a sworn enemy.

I hurried to the Suite Night and gobbled down a six-pack of Eskimo Cheese Whips in a very respectable time.

I figured that Chief York might've had me tailed. I looked out the window. Light snow was coming down at an angle. No one was peeking in.

I flung myself on the bed and read Slim Twitchle's latest column. Laurel was offering a $10,000 reward for the return of some 'confidential files' that had been stolen over the weekend. *Good.* It meant that Laurel hadn't hidden the procedures, someone had taken them.

I called Bill. My nerves tensed with each ring. When the machine answered, I hung up. He should have returned home by now, unless he'd gone into hiding. Or blew his cover on Beezil's hunt, in which case he might be a fresh ingredient in the food chain.

I read the three confidential reports I'd lifted from Laurel. The first was from The Food and Drug Administration. It stated, "Compared to contemporary biological techniques, animal testing is crude, cumbersome, and misleading. Stress and fatigue of isolation and laboratory life grossly distort reactions. Therefore it is not possible to extrapolate results

The second report, mostly formulas and data, concluded: "There are more reliable results from methods such as cell cultures, chemical tests and computer modeling than from animal testing."

By the time I'd finished reading the third report, I was on the verge of needing to breathe into a paper sack. It basically concluded that you probably shouldn't drink Thalo Green nail polish or pour it into your eyes. Handwritten in the margins was: "Results modified to conclude more testing is necessary to determine toxicity levels. Apply for more NIH grants—they have $4 billion to give away this year."

Tomorrow I'll deliver these reports to Slim Twitchle. When he sees the confidential stamp, nothing will stop him from publishing them.

The reports reminded me of the failure to find the test procedures. Which reminded me of my failure to find out who shot Richard, my failure to connect emotionally with Ann, and somehow, every failure in my life. I decided to use the energy born of my frustration to straighten my room. Big mistake. I made a royal mess out of putting the potato chips back inside their bag because I kept squeezing my hand into a fist and squashing whatever chips I held.

When the telephone rang, I punched the receiver off the base. In a commanding voice, Chief York said, "Come to the station. We have a break in the case."

I shouldn't have fallen for it. Not after all I've fallen for in my life.

"Yes ma'am. Be right there." I couldn't remember having given her my phone number. *Let's see. First, I'll notify the press to meet me at the station. Then, when I'm asked to identify the gunman, I'll keep everyone in suspense. I'll dramatically stare at each suspect in the lineup, slowly shake my head, then glare until the gunman's fidgety movements escalate into uncontrollable shivers—and he confesses. Then I'll find myself a good agent for the talk shows.*

I called the Holiday Inn and asked for Slim Twitchle. He

wasn't in his room so I left a message for him to meet me at the police station. Not that I wanted to do him any favors, but when the gunman was booked and the A.L.F. was cleared I wanted Boston to know all about it. I also wanted to give Slim the confidential Laurel papers.

I called Ann and asked her to watch Hoover and Alice. Then I pulled down the window shade and started getting dressed. Snow was blowing hard against the window. While I was putting on my underwear there was a knock at the door, and the window shade snapped up. Two pigeons on the ledge were facing me. One cackled.

"Just a minute." I pulled the shade down again and finished getting dressed.

When I opened the door, Ann stepped inside. She wore a dress covered with a print of big white poppies with round yellow centers. It looked as if she had been pelted with fried eggs. She sat gracefully on the couch.

The telephone rang. When I picked it up, the line went dead.

As I sat across from Ann, the phone rang again. This time I ignored it.

Ann drew her legs up under her. She reminded me of a cat, completely at ease, yet hiding the tension of a coiled spring.

"Where are you going?"

"The police caught the gunman. They want me to identify him."

"But you *can't* identify him."

"True. But the gunman doesn't know that."

"Chief York does."

Also true. So why does she want me at the station?

The phone was still ringing. I looked at Ann, who shrugged. I crossed the room.

"That pesky Madonna, she can't seem to get enough of me."

Hoover, near the phone, heard me approaching and blew

air out of his nostrils as if to say, "It's about time you answered it. . . ."

"Hello," I said. Silence. "Hello?" A muffled male voice spoke so low that I jammed the phone into my ear.

"If you want to know who shot Richard, meet me at Union Street and Jefferson Avenue at nine p.m."

"Nine? Why not tell me now?"

"It needs to be at nine."

"Deal. Nine. But please wait for me if I'm late." I couldn't resist. "Shall I dress casual?"

He answered by suggesting I do something that, well, if I could do what he suggested, I would never leave my room. Then I heard a humming sound in D-flat. The phone line. I went back, sat across from Ann, and told her about the strange call.

Ann reached over and touched my arm.

"Don't go, Clark. It sounds like a trap."

I appreciated her concern. "Okay."

"Just like that? I had this vision of you trying to out-trap the trapper."

I smiled at her. "Magnum always has a fancy scheme when somebody snarling through a rag calls and says to meet him in a bad neighborhood on the far side of town. I don't have *any* scheme."

"But you told him you might be late." She was beginning to grin, too.

"If he's going to waste my time, the least I can do is waste a little of his. And I have the satisfaction of imagining him hanging around a street corner, maybe getting beat up by some drug dealers." It was 5:05 by the upside down Timex on Ann's wrist. "I'd better get to the police station."

"How long will you be gone?"

"Red tape is like flypaper; I could be stuck for hours. Will you feed Alice and Hoover?"

"My pleasure." Ann leaned over and kissed my cheek. Floundering, I searched the coffee table for something to rearrange. There was only a tin ashtray, so I went for that, turning it in bashful circles.

I wanted to tell Ann that she meant a lot to me. My jaws worked, but the words stuck fast to the roof of my mouth.

"I, uh, like your dress."

***

Outside the police station, I heard distant church bells playing Holy Night. Inside, it was silent until the Oriental receptionist snapped open a compact and began examining herself in small oblong patches.

As I approached the Chief's office I could hear her talking. When I reached her door she said into a telephone, "He's here now." She hung up and hastily slid the file she'd been reading under a stack of other files, then made a fuss over all the papers on her desk, curiously in desperate need of rearrangement.

I settled in the chair in front of her. She appeared as if she hadn't had much sleep. Bags drooped under her eyes and her lipstick was smudged sideways, forming a crimson crescent with a distinct bias to the right, making her look like a demented clown. I decided not to mention it. She wasn't that fond of me to begin with.

"Speaking for the Cavalry Police Department," she said, "thank you for helping us bring a criminal to justice." Her eyes looked as though they were laughing at a private joke.

"The fingerprints on the dart I gave you probably belong to a *trigger* man," I said coolly, "not the *brains* of the operation."

Chief York removed handcuffs out of the top drawer and laid them on the desk in the way a suspicious poker player might lay a revolver on the table before the deal. There would be no nonsense here, or I'd be arrested for obstruction of justice.

"Au contraire."

I was certain she had it wrong. I tried not to smirk.

"Thanks to you," she said, "I will make an arrest shortly. We've identified fingerprints at the scene of the crime that shouldn't have been there."

"I thought you wanted me to identify Richard's gunman."

The Chief looked down her nose at me.

"I'm talking about Lester's killer."

Then why call me in? What mental compost pile are you rooting around in now? What's that look in your eye?

In her eyes I began to see the picture: the fingerprints were Bill's, and she was taking me hostage to flush him out.

"Whose prints?"

Chief York leaned over the desk and looked at me, real close so I had to look her right in her eyes, because her eyes, dancing to a heavy beat, filled my field of vision.

"You are under arrest."

I doubt the English language holds a more distressing combination of words than "You are under arrest" (I must concede something to the phrase, "We interrupt your regular programming for a Presidential election update. . . .").

A few minutes later I was breathing normally again.

"Me?"

"You."

"Me?" I repeated. Then, hurrying to correct the impression I was a moron, I said, "Who?"

This, of course, did not improve things.

"You. Now, if you're asking why—"

I brushed my hands through the air.

"Please. Just a second. Let me adjust to being kicked in the face here." I shut my eyes. "Yes. Why?"

"Your fingerprints were all over the lab where Lester was killed."

I was stunned. Elmer's glue should have covered my fingerprints while I was in Laurel. The glue must have come off when I yanked on that ratcheted window.

The Chief had more surprises. "Since Richard was shot with a similar shotgun, and since you had access to Richard's office, I'm betting you were involved in his shooting, as well."

I scooted my chair forward. "As they say in massage

26

parlors, 'Hold everything!' During Richard's attack, I have an alibi, a witness" —I stretched it a bit— "my girlfriend. When Richard was shot, we were sitting on the back of a reporter in the Lobster's parking lot! Call her, please!"

The Chief's voice grew icicles.

"And what is the name of this young lady whose taste, at the moment, is very much in question?"

"Ann Berlin. She'll corroborate my alibi."

"Ann Berlin," the Chief repeated as though trying to place a familiar name. "Granting she backs your story, it still won't provide an alibi, because the shotgun was rigged to fire automatically with a sound-activated device."

That explained why I'd never seen a gunman leaving the Lobster—he'd come and gone. If my life were a cartoon, a light bulb would have appeared above my head. "My fingerprints, you say?" I pulled myself up a little taller. "You mean, you found *Barney Rubble's* fingerprints at the scene of the crime. The name I gave you."

"Your fingerprints, *Mr. Clark Baker.*" She let this revelation sink in, perhaps enjoying whatever facial expression resulted from my stomach feeling as if it had collapsed like a stomped-on Dixie cup. "I lifted your fingerprints off the ceramic cigarette case you so kindly passed to me on your first visit."

I swallowed hard. That explained why she'd handled the cigarette case so gingerly.

"How'd you match my prints?"

"I figured you for a Fluke groupie, so I checked your prints in Fluke's hometown. The police faxed the name that matched your prints, along with your personal data sheet and photo."

With cold grey eyes, she gazed into my face. I imagined she knew everything about me. I shifted a little on the chair (although some might say I squirmed).

"Did you check the prints on the steel dart I gave you?"

"Those belonged to Harry Hickabob. Can you explain why one of Lester's employees was trying to kill you?"

Actually, he seemed mostly to want to delay me and I have no idea why.

"Can't even guess? Well, I think a jury will find it compelling evidence of a feud, and a motive sufficient for you to have murdered Lester." She opened the stenciled file and handed me a typed confession that she wanted me to sign unprotestingly, like an innocent, trusting calf being led through the door at "Oscar Mayer."

"What's wrong, Mr. Baker?"

"Why would I shoot Richard, my friend? And my employer." I started to say just 'Richard, my friend' but added 'and my employer' in case she didn't have any friends. "What was my motive for shooting him? It doesn't make sense!"

"Murder has little to do with sense. It has to do with obsession."

"But I didn't do it," I whined like any normal two-year-old. "Where did you find the shotgun?"

"Doctors told us the pellets entered Richard's body on a downward path, which we traced to the rafters. The shotgun was tied to a crossbeam."

The rafters! Sheesh! I had deduced the gunman was tall. "How could *I* have rigged a shotgun to fire automatically? I mean, I'm not mechanically inclined. I'm dazzled by the concept of Kleenex; draw one out, and another pops up! Magic!"

Her sigh told me how much she accepted that alibi.

"Do you think just because Cavalry is small, the police are country bumpkins?" The words were playful but the meaning was not.

I didn't even consider answering.

She removed the cigarette from her mouth and jabbed it in my direction.

"Time to confess. And try to look a shade less green, will you? It's not your color." She shoved the confession sheet across the desk, then read me my rights.

"Call a lawyer, if you think it'll help." She picked up the

telephone and plunked it down in front of me so hard that it gave out a brief ring of complaint. I stared at it catatonically. She offered me the receiver.

I felt like I was sinking in quicksand and she was offering me a breath mint.

I held out my palm and the Chief dropped the receiver into it. I dialed the Suite Night and while the phone was ringing, I asked the Chief, "Exactly what did you mean by 'the shotgun was rigged to fire automatically'?"

She must have assumed I was playing innocent just to piss her off. She closed her eyes and went tight all over. For a brief happy moment I thought she was going to have a stroke. Instead, she said, "The shotgun was triggered by a sound-activated device taped under Mr. Tipton's desk."

The desk clerk at the Suite Night finally answered with a yawn. I said, "Room 300, please." The phone rang again. Ann answered.

I lowered my voice hoping to disguise the panic in it. "Ann?"

"Clark! You okay?"

"Like a duck in orange-sauce. The police are about to throw me in jail for shooting Lester and Richard."

"Are you joking?"

"I will explain to you, as my lawyer, when you get here."

The Chief puffed a cigarette as she said, "Knowing Judge Silvers, tell your lawyer to bring about two hundred fifty grand to cover bail."

Air escaped from me as though my lungs had been pierced.

Ann had heard the Chief.

"I'll try to get it."

I doubted she could get a quarter million dollars. Most of our friends were rock musicians with financial portfolios consisting primarily of discount pizza coupons. And, judging from the old Dodge that Ann had borrowed, none of her friends needed a forklift to carry their bankbook.

"In the meantime," Ann raised her voice, "tell the Chief

everything." She hung up. I realized, too late, that she probably hadn't heard the correct dollar amount of the bail, since the Chief was puffing while speaking.

I handed the phone back to the Chief. I sensed in her the growing embryo of belief in my story.

Perhaps now is a good time to offer her a bribe. What is the going rate nowadays for bribing a policeman? Does a Chief cost extra? Is there a discount for cash?

That's when I became aware of a police officer who had entered the room without my noticing him. The Chief called the officer "Stubby." Even though he was about six-foot-six inches tall, Stubby's arms seemed too long for his body. He pulled me up out of the chair, spun me around, twisted my elbow up over my head, then muscled me forward.

What the heck, might as well go with him.

He forced me out of the Chief's office and through the hall, but let me go down the stairs under my own power. Probably my reward for going along meek as a lamb. But I had a feeling if I'd resisted at all, he'd have bounced me down every step.

In the basement, cops who moments ago seemed preoccupied, found time to glare at me like I had crawled up out of a sewer. Stubby escorted me to a table and jabbed my fingers onto an ink pad. Someone took my picture.

I was led back upstairs, past the receptionist (tossing down her nail file and picking up a buffer), through a door, and down a row of cells. Our footfalls seemed loud. The only other sounds were snoring from one cell and a low chuckle from another.

After passing a dozen overcrowded cells, a soft voice from a cell ahead called out, "How's Hoover?" Two slender hands were sticking out through the cell bars.

I smiled at a woman dressed in what looked like a negligee, but was probably a silk dress. "Hi, Joy. Hoover's fine, thanks." I lowered my voice. "What'd they nab you for?"

The little-girl timbre of her voice dropped a throaty notch

or two. "Providing my pastor with a lot of sermon topics."
Oh.

Stubby nudged me forward. I nodded to Joy.

"See you."

It wasn't fair. Neither Joy nor I belonged in jail. The justice system was out of whack. I knew from watching television how it was supposed to work. If you were one of the good guys, you would end up chatting and laughing with attractive people on a tropical beach when the program ended. Whereas, bad guys were catapulted in a flaming car into a brick wall.

Stubby opened the door to a cell that held two guys who looked as if their spare time had been devoted to reading girlie magazines and looking through peep holes. *How can they lock me in a cell with these degenerates? Oh yeah. I keep forgetting. The Chief doesn't like me very much.*

For the next several hours I sat with my two cell mates on a hard bench, like three Kewpie dolls in a row. I worked on my prospective defense to the jury: *"Ladies and gentlemen, I couldn't possibly have rigged a shotgun to fire automatically. I will bring to the stand reliable witnesses who will testify I can barely operate a shower curtain."*

Stiffly, I stood and walked to the cell door. In the cell across from me a drunk tried to yodel, but his voice cracked. He began to cry. Life hadn't rewarded his hopes and dreams. He wasn't alone in that, of course, but he seemed to be taking it particularly hard. While thinking about his pain, and how deep it must run, I saw Chief York coming down the hall.

"Chief. If you let me out, I'll never again ask you for a date."

"In that case, you're free to go."

Although it seemed unbelievable, when she opened the door, I squeezed out, turned, and gave my cell mates a farewell grin, enjoying their open-mouthed expressions.

"Bail has been guaranteed," the Chief whispered with her head lowered sadly, I sensed for all humanity.

Joy, three cells away, said good-bye and gave me the kind of wave where you hold your hand still and wiggle your fingers.

As I waved back, my attention was diverted to a commotion in the lobby, where someone hollered, "Who's head of this maggot pile?" The receptionist said, "You can't go in there."

Slim Twitchle put a sidestep move on the receptionist that would have done even O.J. Simpson proud. It left her with a handful of air and eyes the size of dinner plates. She took the defeat well, throwing up her hands in despair.

"You're a crude, slow-leak asshole." When angered, the oriental doll had a strong Brooklyn accent.

Over his shoulder, Slim responded, "If I were a vain person, I'd resent that. Fortunately for me, I'm a spiteful one." He burst down the corridor with a tape recorder and microphone in hand. He stopped at a cell and was prompting a prisoner to air a grievance about being treated unfairly.

An idea popped into my head.

"I was wrongfully imprisoned."

"I do my best," the Chief said.

I nodded to Slim. "Recognize him?"

"Badge says PRESS, but I don't know him."

"He's Slim Twitchle of the *Beacon Hill Examiner*."

"I've heard of him. A prize shit."

"Olympic gold."

The Chief's expression clouded. "What's he doing here?"

"Looking for a story. He can turn a church bazaar into a sordid scandal. Who knows what he can do with wrongful imprisonment. . . ." Slim was ten yards away, his snaky eyes taking in the Chief and me.

The Chief stepped in front of me. "You can't do this!"

"I can even do it with a smile. But I won't—if you release Joy."

The Chief managed to look bewildered and aghast and angry and superior all at the same time. If I got a chance, I would ask her how she did that. She licked her lower lip, then nodded agreement a split second before Slim's microphone jumped on her face like a second nose. "Why was Mr. Baker arrested?"

I stepped between Slim and the Chief.

"Speeding, and for resisting arrest."

Slim pushed the microphone into my face.

"False arrest?"

"No."

"Police brutality?"

I turned my head so he could see the gash on my ear.

"Snap a photo."

Slim plucked a camera from his pocket and snapped a picture so close-up that my ear probably looked like the artwork of Freddie Krueger.

"What's the story?"

"This is the gruesome result of using the *new-and-improved* Terrig razor blade."

Slim knew he'd been duped and practically stamped his foot in vexation.

I reached into my jacket pocket and handed him the three confidential research reports I'd heisted from Laurel.

"I think you'll find these interesting."

Slim read the titles, saw the *confidential* stamp, whistled softly, thanked me, and scurried away.

My hand on the lobby door, I turned to the Chief.

"Thanks."

She politely responded "you're welcome", but I knew the notion of releasing Joy annoyed her, even if she wouldn't have kept Joy long anyway. When I closed the door, I heard her kick the wall and say shit shit shit shit.

The receptionist hollered through the door, "You okay, Chief?"

"I'm all aglow. It's the lucky criminal I catch tomorrow."

* * *

I was a free man. I walked from the police station slowly and with dignity. I jumped as high as I could and knocked an icicle from an awning of the Vinyl Fetish. I winked at the mannequin, sang harmony with two winos warbling "Dashing through the Dough," and helped a homeless lady drag a stunted, distorted Christmas tree that I was pretty sure Joyce Kilmer had never seen.

I looked at my watch: nine p.m. Some poor sucker was waiting for me at Union Street and Jefferson Avenue. He'd regret having played games with me. He'd know now that I was as devious as he; that my brain wasn't a chew toy or something I took out and played with.

Life was good.

In the recesses of my mind a revelation started gnawing through. Something the Chief had said. No. No . . . no . . . YES! The gunman had used a sound-activated device. An electronic bug.

Lester had been an electronics expert in the military. If Ransacker worked for Lester, and planted a bug in my room during his first break-in, it would explain why nothing was stolen. It would also explain how The Rat knew when to attack me in the alley, and how Mungo knew when to break into the Suite Night.

If he wanted me gone now, was he planning to break in again?

I ran to a phone booth and called my room. It rang ten, twelve, fourteen times. Ann didn't pick up.

Am I too late? I caught sight of myself in the cracked glass of the phone booth. My hair was disheveled, my cheeks flushed, my eyes bulging. I looked like a man in emotional shock. A caricature of myself.

A taxi approached. Considering the frantic way I hailed it the driver didn't dare *not* stop. At the Suite Night I threw him some money, and bolted through the lobby. Outside my room I heard Hoover waddling around. I opened the door. Hoover wagged his tail and yelped and flung himself about so joyfully that when I went to pat him, I missed. Alice hopped out from under the bed.

I knocked on Ann's door. No answer.

I looked out the window and saw Mungo in a car at the end of the alley, listening to what I guessed was a receiver. On the backseat was a silver fox fur coat, probably the coat Lester had worn the night Richard was shot.

I started searching my room for Lester's bug. To cover up the sounds of moving furniture, I whistled. Hoover listened, his expressive face worried.

"It's a beautiful day, okay?" Hoover leaned against my leg the way he leans when he's nervous.

Then his ears pricked alert and he cocked his head. He growled softly. I heard someone scrambling up the stairwell.

I raced to lock the door.

Mungo smashed through it, sending me reeling backwards. I tripped over my suitcase and crashed hard to the floor, head first. A deep pool of darkness opened and I started to dive in. I wanted to yell at Hoover to run away, but I couldn't. I had no will, only eyes, as in a dream. I blacked out.

Then shock waves rippled the pool of darkness. Sound. Hoover was barking. The darkness shimmered, hazy variable light, then my eyes focused.

Mungo landed a hard kick on Hoover's side, splaying him to the ground. When Mungo shifted his weight for another kick, I tried to tackle him. He turned and clotheslined me, then grabbed my throat.

I yelled but no sound escaped. His hand pressed so hard against my throat I could barely breathe. Then he suddenly let go, stepped behind me, and picked me up in a bear hug.

"Where are they?"

"Where are what?"

"The test procedures worth ten-grand."

"I don't know." I tried to squirm away, but he clutched me like a beast with a death grip on its prey and carried me toward the fire escape.

"Give 'em to me," Mungo said, "or you'll have a bad accident—ahhh, shit!" Mungo tried to shake his leg but Hoover's teeth were sunk deep into his ankle. Mungo stumbled. I broke free and scrambled away. Mungo grabbed for me and lost his balance. I watched in horror as he landed on Hoover.

Hoover squealed and lay still.

Mungo started to get up but I'd already grabbed my suitcase and was swinging it in a giant roundhouse. The steel corner cracked over Mungo's skull. He clutched his head, listed left, then toppled.

Hoover shuddered violently and groaned.

"You okay?" My voice was raspy. Hoover and I sounded like the same species.

He tried feebly to stand. I patted his head to settle him, but he got up and limped toward the door, put his paws up on the wall and pointed to his leash.

"I'm not sure we should leave him."

I took Hoover's leash, tied Mungo's arms behind him,

then wrestled him over to the refrigerator. I wrapped a guitar string around his ankles and twisted the ends together. I didn't know exactly what kind of knot to tie, so I tied a lot of them. I looped an E-string, the thinnest and sharpest, loosely around Mungo's neck, and tied the other end to the fridge door.

I called Dr. Dean and explained that Hoover was hurt. Before I finished telling him that I didn't have a car, he said his son was on the way.

After tightening the knots, I said, "Wake up." Mungo didn't stir. I kicked his right shoe. He stiffened, one eye fell open, then closed, and he settled again. I grabbed his ears and shook his head. His eyes popped open, and in them was a frightening emptiness.

He squirmed and tried to pull his feet up under him. The E-string tightened around his throat, and he slowly sat back down.

"Who hired you to shoot Richard?"

He wasted enough bad language in ten seconds to last an ordinary man all his life, with care. I caught him by surprise with a hard backhand on his left cheek.

Then I waited for him to talk.

A cold grey light glinted in his eyes.

I slapped him hard on the right cheek.

"I can keep this up forever."

"Oh, can you? You'd have to damn near kill me before I'd tell you anything, and you haven't got the guts."

I cocked my backhand. He didn't wince. It was ludicrous. I had the cretin tied up, and he was in control of the situation.

Hoover's head trembled as he licked blood from his paw. Alice was curled up next to him. I bent down and stroked Hoover, trying to calm and reassure him. Or maybe myself.

"Let me go," Mungo said, "and maybe I won't turn the A.L.F. names over to the cops. If you don't, all of you, even that damned ugly spider, will go to jail."

That reminded me. *Mungo hates bugs.*

I went to the blender. Smuffy and I exchanged vulnerable, searching looks. Carefully, I tilted the blender and put my fingers inside. Smuffy crawled into my palm with the deliberate high steps of a show horse. I carried her over to Mungo.

Mungo's eyes bulged out of his head like soft-boiled eggs in eggcups, either trying to see more clearly, or maybe simply trying to leave. He leaned away, and the wire noose tightened.

I put my hand by his shoulder, and Smuffy climbed onto it. Mungo started to shake. Smuffy moved slowly toward Mungo's neck—just as Mungo's hand had crept down Ann's neckline. My anger built.

"You shake, she'll bite."

Mungo stiffened against the fridge like a man being electrocuted. His tough façade gone.

"Last chance," I said. Smuffy extended her front legs, feeling Mungo's neck.

Mungo's eyes were wild, close to hysteria. Almost imperceptibly he nodded. I pressed my open hand against one of the pale sweaty rings in his neck, just below Smuffy. She crawled into my palm. I put her back into the blender and blood started coming back to Mungo's face.

"Talk."

"You know Purple-Hair, the fuzznut who jumped onto the stage? After he got bounced, he snuck back in with a sawed-off shotgun—"

I banged his head backward against the fridge, hard enough to knock over a jar inside.

"Damn you. Listen to me. Someone planted a full-size shotgun in the rafters. You don't know how much I know, so it's a bad time to try lying. The only way you could know I called Brett 'Purple-Hair' is because you've been eavesdropping. Where did you plant the bug?"

Mungo clenched his jaw and stared at me.

I reached back into the blender, waited for Smuffy to

crawl onto my hand, and let her off again high on Mungo's neck. Mungo's whole body flexed. For a moment I thought he might be strong enough to snap the steel wires. He wasn't. Instead, the wires seemed to bite through his flesh.

As Smuffy crawled over his chin, Mungo shut both his eyes. With each step, Mungo bent his head back, until he was facing the ceiling. Smuffy crawled over Mungo's cheek, nestled into his right eye socket, and then settled like she might go to sleep.

I pulled a loose splinter of wood off the door frame and poised it, ready to prod her to bite. I hesitated. I hated to poke her after she trusted me to handle her. Now I was sweating.

Hoover seemed to understand. But whether he did or not, he suddenly sprang onto his hind legs, leaning his forepaws on Mungo for support, and barked. Smuffy bit into Mungo's scrunched eyelid.

"Christ! Get me a doctor!" His fingers were digging into the refrigerator.

Hoover dropped his forepaws to the ground.

"Ready to talk?"

Mungo nodded his head feverishly, although it was no more than a tremor.

I called the police. "Can you get here right away? I have someone who will confess to trying to kill Richard Tipton."

***

"Let me go," Mungo demanded.

Strolling to the window, Chief York asked, "Why?"

"Because I didn't do anything wrong! Untie me!"

Grief suddenly filled me as I realized I'd made a tragic mistake. I was new at detective work, and I had forgotten to get any proof. *The police will have to let this killer go free. Were I any dumber, I'd have to be watered.*

"Untie me," Mungo growled.

"We didn't tie you up," the Chief said. "Whatever two people do in the privacy of their own hotel room is their own business. Isn't that right, Stubby?"

Now wait just one lousy minute—

"That's right." Stubby rubbed his fingers along the guitar strings binding Mungo to the refrigerator. "And, quite frankly, we've seen a lot kinkier than this."

"I want to press charges," Mungo glared from me to Smuffy. "That madman put a poison spider on my face. My eyelid is swelling. Take me to a doctor!"

The Chief shook her head.

"No, sir. We're not an ambulance service. We *can* take you to jail, but only if we have a reason to arrest you."

"Jesus Herbert Christ! You're saying if I don't confess, you'll leave me here?"

"Absolutely correct, however, you get no points because I had to give you a hint." Stubby turned, hiding his smile.

Mungo strained forward against the steel wires. "Very funny. Okay. I'll tell you who shot Richard if you get me to a doctor!"

"Promises, promises." Chief York watched the pigeons outside on the ledge, conveying to Mungo he'd have to work harder to hold her interest.

"Okay," Mungo said. "Here's what I know . . ."

"First things first," the Chief turned, rested her fanny on the windowsill, folded her arms, then read Mungo his rights.

The formalities out of the way, Mungo began, "Lester brought a shotgun into the Lobster under a fur coat. Then he hid it in the rafters of Richard's office while Kat and I argued with Dudley and Richard about a 'reserved' booth. For the love of Jesus, get me outta here."

"Did Beezil hire you to kill Richard?" I asked.

"No," Mungo said. "Beezil only wanted Fluke out of town. It was Lester's idea to use the shotgun to close the Lobster."

"Then why'd you attack Mr. Baker and Miss Berlin *after* Fluke left town?"

"A story in the *Examiner* said Clark was after the gunman. Lester wanted to know how much Clark knew, so he had me bust into this dump and hide a bug. I made it look like a burglary to confuse Clark."

"Why'd you leave a key in my door?" I asked.

"Mr. Terrig knew the insurance company wouldn't pay him until after an investigation, which might prove it was arson and get the police involved. So he gave me a key to cleaning fluid cabinets near the furnace and asked me to plant it on someone. I stuck it in your hotel door, hoping you'd keep it."

Doubt crossed the Chief's face.

"Why did you break in a second time?"

"To put new batteries in the bug," Mungo said, "and confuse Clark more. I knew from listening that if I broke in that night, he'd believe someone had seen him at the Lobster."

The Chief asked, "Where's the bug?"

"Under the couch."

I asked, "Why did you want me gone at nine o'clock?"

"That's when the desk clerk takes his nap. I was waiting for him to nod off when you came home."

The Chief whispered to Stubby: "Check under the couch. Be very quiet. The bug could trigger something to explode." The Chief looked at the counter. "We could end up looking like that bag of chips."

Stubby nodded. His face rigid with intent, he advanced on the couch. As he tipped it slowly backward, I shifted my feet and flexed my knees in position to dive at the first sound. Stubby spotted the bug and studied it while balancing the couch.

"It's safe." Stubby gripped it by two thin wires and handed it to the Chief.

Stubby and the Chief stepped into the living room. I followed them.

"Do we have enough to convict him?" Stubby asked.

"He's confessed only to keeping people busy while Lester planted the shotgun. That's accessory. But he's quick to blame Lester for everything, so I'd bet he knows Lester is dead."

"We need to find the other shotgun."

I cleared my throat. Their stares could have nailed me to the wall.

I said, "It's on the backseat of Mungo's car, right outside. Car's probably unlocked, he left in a hurry."

Stubby went to the car and returned with the shotgun.

Mungo swallowed hard and his swollen eyelid twitched spastically.

"Okay. Okay. After Kristin died, Brett leaked crap to Terrig about the upcoming Laurel raid. Terrig wanted to catch the guys responsible for Kristin's death, so he convinced John Laurel to hire a dude who would protect Laurel. He said he knew of a 'recovering' animal-rights puke who knew the A.L.F.'s tactics and who wanted revenge.

"This puke didn't really exist. Terrig's plan was to have Lester hiding inside Laurel and videotape A.L.F. members. Then he'd blackmail them. He and Lester were in agreement— all for one, one for all—until Ann and Clark visited the Terrigs. Then Terrig changed his mind, took back his cameras a few hours before the raid, and told Lester to stop guarding Laurel. But Lester had a plan: shoot video and sell it to Slim Twitchle. He asked me to bring him a camera, but I needed time. So Rat delayed you in the alley, using the toy helicopter."

That explains why he only delayed us. In fact, he wanted us to continue with the break-in. "How did he get our Cobra?"

"Lester heard about your car wreck from Terrig, who heard it from Brett. We went and checked it out."

"Why?"

"Looking for heroin needles or other contraband carried by rockers. Or the list of A.L.F. members. Anything to black-mail you with."

"Interesting," Stubby said, "but why kill Lester?"

Mungo's expression was bewildered, the eyes affronted, blaming, like the eyes of a caught fish. "When I took the cameras to Lester, I told him it wasn't smart to double-cross Terrig. But he'd been drinking," Mungo wrinkled his brow.

"Although I don't know where he got the beer. Anyway, we argued and he told me to kill all the rabbits. I didn't know how plastered he was. When I hesitated, he got mad, pumped his rifle and yelled at me to kill the rabbits or he'd feed me to them. He pinched my cheek like I was a little kid." Mungo looked pained, like a knife was stuck in him. "I punched him. While he was falling backward, I grabbed the rifle. The blast drove him into a chair." Mungo made a wrenching sound that masked my sigh of relief. Bill had not killed Lester.

Stubby untied Mungo, helped him to his feet, cuffed him, and directed him out the door. Mungo's knees buckled. If Stubby hadn't been holding him, he would have gone down the stairs like a runny egg. "Think now we have enough to convict him?" Stubby asked.

The Chief almost giggled. Mungo, babbling piteously, was confessing to sins he had committed all the way back in the fifth grade.

After I filled out paperwork in Chief York's office, I said good-bye and thanked her.

She nodded to her door, which was open a crack, allowing us a sliver view of Ann in the lobby. "I might have listened better had I known you kept such top-notch company. I thought I recognized her name when you said it. I've seen Ms. Berlin get children out of abusive situations. I wish more lawyers were like her."

Ann was sitting on a wooden bench, reading a book as if she'd always been there. Her posture was breathtaking. I watched her, wanting to keep the portrait forever. One day in the future, because I loved her, I would unveil it for her.

When our eyes met, she rose gracefully, closing the book without marking her place. I was something out of the Three Stooges—nine or ten people stood between us, and I left footprints on maybe six of them.

Without my customary restraint, I gathered her into my arms.

"Thanks for being here."

We held each other around the waist and locked eyes. Ann smiled. Gradually, I looked at the other people.

Dominating the east end of the lobby were Chas and Petey. Chas stepped forward and hugged me. I felt as if I were being rolled up in a king size feather mattress.

"Did you know your great aunt was back in town?" I said.

He looked confused. "Aunt Edith? Edith is back?" I gave him the address. He ran out with Petey, almost knocking Corky down.

Corky's arm was looped through Dudley's, her hair looked as if she'd sprayed it with Easy-Off and beat it into place with the *Wall Street Journal*.

"Hi." Her eyes, bright with merriment, as usual told more than did her words.

Dudley said, "Bill and I teamed up and retrieved the rabbit test procedures."

My mouth dropped open.

"When?"

"An hour before the liberation kicked off."

"Why did you break rank?"

Bill was standing behind Richard who was in a wheelchair.

"On Mr. Terrig's hunt I made some friends. I was talking with one just before the Laurel mission. He'd heard Lester was guarding Laurel. So Dudley and I devised a reconnaissance mission and quickly executed it."

"How'd you slip past Lester?"

Bill raised his baseball cap to me. His head was shaved, recklessly, as if he'd used a dull cheese grater.

"I knocked on the side door of Laurel. When Lester answered, I dangled a 6-pack of Body Slam Malt Liquor just out of his reach while I spewed long Biblical passages."

As only you can, brother Bill.

"While Bill preached at the side door," Dudley said, "I used the A.L.F.'s key to the front door. I found a file cabinet marked 'Test Procedures' and carted out eight boxes of files. Since I didn't know if they contained the incriminating procedures, I didn't tell anyone. I took the boxes to Corky."

Bill said, "I delivered the last van to Laurel, then climbed onto a nearby roof to scout for police. When Laurel's burglar alarm sounded and the police came, I dropped Corky's 'screaming for help' tape into a trash bin."

I threw a mental bouquet to my brother.

"Dudley and I searched through the boxes of files," Corky said. "When we found the test procedures I was so happy, I started crying. I wasn't conscious of Dudley embracing me until I felt him weeping on my neck."

Dudley's strong chiseled features blushed cherry blossom pink.

Corky continued, "Before I knew it we were laughing. We've been together ever since."

Bill stood next to Mr. and Mrs. Terrig.

"Bill," I said, "you made friends on the hunt?"

"You bet. Mr. Terrig didn't go, but fifteen others did. I told jokes and kept everyone laughing while we hiked through the woods. I shot five-hundred rounds into dead tree stumps. Wore a strong cologne and blew a warning whistle only animals would hear. After sixteen hours nobody had killed anything, but the Rednecks invited me back, promising they would do better next time."

"The Terrigs called everyone here to make amends," Ann said. "Besides, they had a vested interest in your arrest. They guaranteed the bail money."

Everyone seemed to think my expression was sidesplitting.

"I'm so glad you're all right," Mrs. Terrig said.

Beezil shook my hand. "I apologize for blaming you for Kristin's death. I guess I needed to blame someone other than myself. I want everyone to know that the Terrig Corporation will no longer be testing products on animals. To honor Kristin's memory, and because after reading all she wrote, I appreciate that all animals, human or not, feel the whip, fight the chain, and grieve for their loved ones."

Mrs. Terrig held out her arms to include us all. "You're all invited to our home for a midnight snack."

Even the receptionist, studying the finish on her perfect manicure, promised to be there.

Bill rolled Richard's wheelchair forward. I put my hand on Richard's shoulder. "You look great. But you sure had us worried, you know that?"

"*You* were worried? One time I woke up and heard a doctor say, 'Where's my lucky scalpel? These gunshot wounds in the groin can be a very serious thing.' I passed out again."

"Where's Hoover?" Ann asked.

"At Dr. Dean's," I said. "Let's go."

* * *

The interior of the cab was warm and smoky and smelled of vomit and pine-scented disinfectant. The plastic barrier between the front and back seats was halfway open. The meter read $3.75. Mounted on the dashboard was a black-and-white mug shot of the cabby.

Hoover, his nose out the right-hand window, was busy enjoying his release from Dr. Dean's.

"His side is swollen," Ann said, "but he doesn't seem to be in pain." She softly punched my shoulder. "You, however, look ghastly. You feeling okay?"

I stroked Hoover's head. "When I sent him to obedience school, he liked it. Now he actually enjoys being tied up and whipped."

"Can't you ever give me a straight answer? Do you have to make fun of everything?"

I shifted in the seat. "Sometime I'll give you my widely-acclaimed lecture on 'How to make fun of income taxes, cancer, and drive-by shootings.'"

Ann turned her head to the window.

The cabby spoke up, "Psychologists maintain that people use humor to avoid dealing with feelings. It's a defense to conceal their emotional vulnerability."

"Really? And how do you suppose psychologists test these theories? Teach lab rats to tell jokes? Dress them in funny little rat-sized clown suits?"

In the reflection of Ann's face in the window I was hoping to see a smile. What I saw was enough anger in her eyes to make them snap.

"It's unhealthy to hold feelings inside," the cabby said.

I've always wondered what happened to those Ph.D.s in psychology.

"Holding feelings inside creates stress," Ann said and glanced in the rearview mirror at the cabby, who gave her a quick nod of agreement.

Then it started. First Ann attacked me, then the cabby attacked me. Even in the brief silences, they somehow remained united. They assured me that I'd be healthier if I expressed more of my feelings.

"Phhhht!" I expressed. "I know I was here, but when, exactly, did this turn into my own personal *roast*?"

They looked at each other. "That comment is exactly like him," Ann said.

The cabby agreed, adding that "phhhht" didn't count as a feeling.

This cabby deserves a tip that shows him what his advice is worth. He's lucky I don't carry expired jars of "I Can't Believe It's Not Jelly."

Yet, I felt a stinging pang of regret for holding in my feelings.

Why can't I tell anyone what I feel? Is this why everyone else is happy and I'm as lonely as an orphan? Of course not. But it explains what happens to people who spend too much time talking to spiders.

My mind felt a peculiar sensation, as though it were sinking back into itself, assuming some mental equivalent of the fetal position. I was inhibited by a reserve that resulted less from shyness than from an acute awareness that I was a damaged man and that Ann deserved someone finer than I could ever be.

She looked at me and I saw, with a chill, that her eyes

were infinitely deep, opening like a tunnel to another universe. Something in them told me I was about to change.

"I'm afraid of change," I said. "Losing the band. Loving and losing. Knowing someday I'll lose Hoover." *And you.*

Hoover pulled his head inside the cab, looked at me curiously, then stuck it outside again.

"I've been afraid of losing loved ones since the death of my dad and my first dog, Kirby. . . ."

Never had I admitted to anyone how much pain I'd felt when Dad died. I'd always kept that pain under my hat. Never had the rational side of my brain allowed the emotional side to assume command. Not since I was nine. Yet, somehow my emotions came pouring out, all the pain kept close, yet covered.

I rambled on about how much I missed Kirby and Dad, talking fast, almost breathless. Speaking of how, if Dad were alive, we'd look at the stars and stay up all night and talk and stand shoulder-to-shoulder and discuss life and philosophy and music and so much more. I told them of how, even now, sometimes I wake before dawn, especially after the Red Sox have won a game in the late innings and I've gone hoarse from screaming, of how I'll think, my mind still fogged with sleep, "I can't wait to talk with Dad about the game." Then I'll reach out to pet Kirby. . . . I told them that this is my cruelest dream.

When I finished, I felt strangely free, yet apprehensive about having changed. I felt, I suppose, like the first fish that grew hands and hauled himself ashore.

Softly, the cabby said, "Often when someone dies those left behind think to themselves, if only I could have one more day: I would use it so well—an hour, perhaps even a minute. You feel guilty for having spent more time with your dog, than with your dad when they were alive. You've spent your entire life feeling guilty about that, trying to prove to yourself, and to others, that animals are the equal of mankind. All so you can justify the feelings you had when you were nine. You'd like the world to say what you felt was okay. Until then, you won't let yourself be part of the world. Until you accept those feelings, you won't get close to another person. Let me be the first to tell you, it's okay to be happy in a world that isn't perfect."

As he drove, the cabby looked at me in the rearview mirror more than he looked through the windshield. But neither Ann nor he picked on me anymore.

By the time we pulled up in front of the Suite Night, the three of us had made up. I gave the cabby fifty dollars and told him to pick up the homeless man who lived in the entranceway of Hammer's, help him with his bags, and bring him back to stay my remaining paid-up days in the Suite Night. *I wish I could see the expression on the face of the desk clerk who turned up his nose at me.*

Ann and I went inside and got Alice. Back outside, once again, words pounded in my heart, trying to escape.

"I love you," I said. Ann gave me a jumbo hug.

"Mama told me this would happen. She said, 'Someday, Clark, you'll meet a girl so special, so perfect for you, that you won't even haggle over price.'"

Ann's laughter rippled out soft and low, as if this particular laugh had been waiting too long.

Hoover wagged his tail, wanting to share our happiness without knowing what it was.

Maybe it isn't happiness until it's shared.

Alice ran out into the snow and looked back at Hoover. Hoover was catching snow in his mouth, but standing still. Alice thumped her foot and Hoover bounced toward her, a swatch of black and white fur in the wind, enjoying the snow as never before.

I was understanding the bigger picture. My father used to say, "If your brain can't make you happy, what good is it? Practice happiness; encourage it. Think of it as an art." For a moment, just a moment, I felt the awesome dimensions of the universe in my heart and held them there, like a secret.

As each moment of the present became the past, my love for Ann grew stronger. And, after a time, or a few times anyway, she fell in love with me.

Coming next: *The Underground Window*

While Clark goes underground to stop a fanatical branch of the A.L.F., Valerie sabotages a hostile takeover attempt of Terrig Corp. When she is kidnapped, there isn't much Clark can do.

* * *

"Let me help you snap out of it," Dudley said. "I'll turn up the television loud enough to make a bombing raid sound like the woodwind section of the London Philharmonic. Loud enough so you can scream."

"No. Please."

"Yes, Clark. Don't hold your emotions in."

"I want to."

"No, Clark. Yell. Bust something. Rip something."

I raised my head. "I'll rip your flapping lips off!"

"All right, then. Do it."

"Coming right up!" I got to my feet, power crowding out my fatigue. "You're about to look as if you're always smiling."

"That's better. Now, let's get something to eat."

* * *

Chez Beagle's owner was a large man with spooked eyes. You wouldn't want to draw his number in a rodeo. And if you didn't know he owned the restaurant, you'd think he was there to rob it. He handed us a menu. Not that we needed one. We could have studied the tablecloth. Apparently, the previous patrons had eaten through it.

"Ann," I said, "what would you do if I murdered him."

"For kidnapping Valerie?"

"Because he threatened to hurt her."

"Before he actually hurts her, you'd kill him?"

"Right. Not in self-defense, but in a calculated, premeditative way, clearing space on my calendar and everything."

"So, is this hypothetical, or have you already gone round the twist?"

"I don't know. I was just thinking about what murder would do to our relationship."